PRAISE FOR
LEADING THE WHOLE TEACHER

In this brilliantly practical and necessary book, Allyson Apsey takes the reader far beyond the technical details of effective instruction. Recognizing the emotional and psychological needs of classroom educators, she gives leaders essential insights on how to improve teacher effectiveness, engage their hearts, and regain their commitment to our profession. At a time when many teachers are burned out and traumatized, Apsey offers hope.

> —**Douglas Reeves, author, *Fearless Schools: Building Trust and Resilience for Learning, Teaching, and Leading***

Allyson Apsey gets it. She sees our pain points and has shown up big-time! With deep credibility and an authentic voice, *Leading the Whole Teacher* will provide you with a clear path to protecting the most important part of education—the people. This book will engage your heart and mind as you serve your staff and school in a manner that's meaningful to them. Our best days in education are ahead, and Allyson Apsey shows us how to get there.

> —**Dr. Brad Gustafson, award-winning principal (MN), author, and speaker**

As a service-oriented leader, Allyson has created a resource that is a necessary addition to the field. *Leading the Whole Teacher* is a book you will keep close to your desk and return to throughout the year.

> —**Jessica Cabeen, principal of Austin Online Academy, author, and speaker**

Leaders lead by example. When I think of powerful leaders in education, Allyson Apsey is one of the first names that comes to my mind. I was blown away by how many great ideas are in *Leading the Whole Teacher*. As leaders, we must embrace, acknowledge, and grow the WHOLE teacher, and Allyson gives you the tools to do just that.

> —**Todd Nesloney, director of culture and strategic leadership at TEPSA, author, and speaker**

Leading the Whole Teacher is a book of empowerment for new and veteran leaders to maximize their ability to lead by creating and facilitating an environment where teachers can enjoy work instead of simply enduring it.

—Hayward Jean, national education speaker, Speak Life Enterprises, director of student services, Orangeburg County School District

During a time of crisis in education, when we are losing educators from our classrooms faster than we can replace them, Allyson provides educational leaders with a roadmap to make our schools places where our educators *want* to work. Through wisdom and practical resources, Allyson does what few educational books are able to do: inspires and guides. Rooted in Dr. Glasser's choice theory and reality therapy, Allyson shows how caring for the whole educator goes beyond self-care and targets all facets of what truly makes our educators essential to the success of our schools.

—Rebekah Schipper, MEd, executive director, Opportunity Thrive

Allyson Apsey has poured her heart and experience into *Leading the Whole Teacher.* In this season of education where teachers are burned out and underappreciated, Allyson gives tangible ideas and strategies to start caring for the educators we have in our buildings. Apsey is vulnerable in her reflections on leadership, missteps she has made, and what she has learned from those moments. She beautifully melds her experience with research to create a blueprint for leaders to start using immediately. Every leader should be reading this book to better support the educators they serve.

—Shane Saeed, educator, national presenter, author of *Be the Flame*

Allyson Apsey writes from the heart with a grounded sense of what teachers need to be successful. Too often, leaders face challenges and aren't able to respond to the heart of the school. Apsey provides clear strategies and considerations for readers to connect, care, and lead.

—Neil Gupta, district administrator, Worthington Schools, Ohio

The demands placed on teachers are overwhelming, and leaders like Allyson Apsey make the impossible seem possible. When teachers are supported as whole individuals within their schools, they are able to focus their efforts on making a difference for each child in their classrooms. In *Leading the Whole Teacher*, Apsey writes from the heart, sharing her own challenges and failures, and inspires all educators to create schools where teachers are able to do their best work because they know they are valued.

—Clint Pulver, Emmy Award-winning keynote speaker and author of the #1 bestselling book *I Love It Here: How Great Leaders Create Organizations Their People Never Want To Leave*

LEADING THE WHOLE TEACHER

LEADING THE WHOLE TEACHER

Strategies for Supporting the Educators in Your School

Allyson Apsey

Leading the Whole Teacher: Strategies for Supporting the Educators in Your School
© 2022 Allyson Apsey

This book is available at special discounts when purchased in quantity for educational purposes or for use as premiums, promotions, or fundraisers. For inquiries and details, contact the publisher at books@daveburgessconsulting.com.

Published by Dave Burgess Consulting, Inc.
San Diego, CA
DaveBurgessConsulting.com

Library of Congress Control Number: 2022943010
Paperback ISBN: 978-1-956306-35-4
Ebook ISBN: 978-1-956306-36-1

Cover design by Sarah Flood-Baumann
Interior design by Liz Schreiter
Edited and produced by Reading List Editorial
ReadingListEditorial.com

This book is dedicated to every person who chose the most impactful profession that exists: education. Thank you for your passion to improve our world through your work with students. Your huge heart is appreciated, and your tireless devotion is noticed.

I also dedicate this book to the three most important people in my life: my husband, Jim, and my sons, Laine and Tyson. I am the luckiest mom and wife in the world to be loved and supported by you. My hope every day is that you know how much I love you.

CONTENTS

CHAPTER 1

REMEMBERING THAT TEACHERS ARE PEOPLE, TOO

Human greatness does not lie in wealth or power, but in character and goodness. People are just people, and all people have faults and shortcomings, but all of us are born with a basic goodness.

—Anne Frank

It's a Tuesday in November and I wake up thinking, "Is my alarm going off already?" That thought may or may not have included a swear word. Shoving my pillow aside and brushing my hair out of my eyes, I remember my goal: to be like Oprah and start each day with gratitude. I swipe at my phone to stop my alarm and quickly reframe my thinking to say a big thank-you for the day ahead.

Rather than getting up and exercising, I'd opted to sleep in. I'd stayed up late responding to texts and emails about an upsetting Facebook post from a parent that was filled with (at best) half-truths. My teachers are hurt, overwhelmed, frustrated, and disappointed, and my heart aches for them. Honestly, it aches for me, too. So often it feels like we can barely come up for air before we're pulled right back down again. So

I slept a bit longer to try to make up for the sleep I lost. And in the process, I skipped my workout. Again.

In general, I try hard not to look at my phone first thing in the morning, but it's lighting up like the Fourth of July. We are short on substitute teachers again. Dang it. When can we catch a break? I take a deep breath and remind myself that this day could go one of two ways: several new substitute teachers might magically appear at our door, or we'll have to cobble together an all-hands-on-deck coverage plan, leaving all of us daydreaming about what a thirty-minute duty-free lunch feels like.

On my drive to work in my messier-than-usual car filled with crumpled receipts and empty Starbucks cups, I try to turn my thinking around by listening to the uplifting playlist I created for mornings such as this. (I also try to convince myself that no one will be able to see the coffee I drip on my shirt.) I am ready for the day. I can do this! Before I even drop my bags in my office, two teachers are at my door saying they have COVID-19 symptoms and need to take a test. At this point, I feel my eyes go wide as saucers while my heart breaks. For me. For them. For all of us. I summon every bit of empathy left in my body to say, "Oh no, I am so sorry. Let me put this stuff down and help you with that."

As I set my stuff down, my phone pings; the Facebook onslaught isn't over yet. My eyes tear up, and I look out the office window for a moment. The pavement is still wet from the rain last night, and kids are avoiding puddles as they step off the bus. The parking lot is starting to buzz with cars going through the drop-off lane. And I realize that the world is going to continue moving. With my whole heart, I want it to move with our team doing great work together. And taking our lunch breaks! This split-second reflection fills me with optimism and resolve. We can do great work together, and we can start taking our lunch breaks. Again.

I share this story at the beginning of this book to make sure you know that I get you. I see you. I share your struggles. And I know that together we can overcome our challenges and do more for teachers than scrape up the last shreds of our empathy. For the past several years, starting way before the pandemic, I have been researching what teachers need to get reconnected to their purpose and to be fulfilled as *whole* people in our profession. I truly believe that we can significantly improve the teacher shortage crisis and substantially improve the working conditions for our current teachers through paying closer attention to the six pillars of the whole teacher, which I'll outline in this book.

What if every teacher felt seen and valued? What if they felt supported by an incredible team who always has their back? How might that change the teacher recruitment and retention crisis we now face? Would our conversations shift from talking about burnout to talking about empowerment? How would the teacher's perception of self change? What would that mean for our students?

Let's allow the data to inform our approach: in April 2019, the Economic Policy Institute reported that "the teacher shortage is real, large and growing, and worse than we thought."[1] And this was before the COVID-19 pandemic that hit in 2020. The report found that 13.8 percent of teachers left their schools or left the profession altogether in the 2011–2012 school year, and it also showed that schools were having a harder time filling vacancies (1). This is not new information for principals who have watched the candidate pool dwindle over the past few years in even the most affluent districts. Of course, the problem is even worse in economically disadvantaged districts. According to the Economic Policy Institute, more teachers are leaving the profession within their first five years, and fewer young adults are leaving college with education degrees (14, 7). To attract young adults into the education profession, we need to be able to offer them the support they need to move from surviving to thriving. The cost of losing teachers is real both in terms of the detriment to student achievement and the financial loss.

---

1 Emma García and Elaine Weiss, "U.S. Schools Struggle to Hire and Retain Teachers," Economic Policy Institute, April 16, 2019, files.epi.org/pdf/164773.pdf, 1.

Shrinking benefits and increasing workplace demands are causing education to lose its appeal for high school seniors considering their career options. Many educators have told me that they are steering their own children away from choosing a career in our field. Gone are the pensions that assure a comfortable retirement. Gone is the top-of-the-line health insurance fully covered by the school district. These perks have been replaced with the reality that teachers not only teach but also act as mental health care providers, trauma-informed experts, and innovators trying to keep up with ever-evolving technology. The reality is that teachers are people, too, and there is only so much they can carry on their shoulders before they break. Seeing that many of their older colleagues, education veterans, are miserable and just waiting for retirement is even more discouraging to young teachers. It's no surprise that they're leaving the field en masse.

The Economic Policy Institute report found that the number of schools trying unsuccessfully to fill a vacancy tripled from the 2011–2012 to 2015–2016 school years (10). It makes sense that the difficulty in filling teaching positions coincided with a significant decrease in the number of education degrees awarded; between 2008 and 2016 there was a 15.4 percent drop in the number of graduates leaving schools with education degrees (8). Again, let's keep in mind that this was before the extra demands placed on teachers during the COVID-19 pandemic.

Not all hope is lost, my friends. As educational leaders, much is out of our control. But many of the most important things are well within our control. We have an opportunity to support the whole teacher by increasing our efforts to match their needs. Every report on teacher retention I've read says the same thing: we need to improve working conditions and job satisfaction to combat the teacher recruitment and retention problems we face. We have a beautiful opportunity here to help our teachers feel strong and powerful. When they know they have a crew of colleagues and leaders supporting them, when they know their own value and areas for growth, they will feel like they can take on any challenge that comes their way.

Every teacher brings their whole self to school: their dreams, their personal challenges, their hopes and fears, and their desire to be valued, to be connected, and to learn and grow. We have a duty to create school environments that can nurture every part of a teacher, that can help them stay connected to their *why*, that can fulfill their servant hearts. We will break down the specific components of the whole teacher in this book and dive into strategies that will help create the environment that teachers need to thrive.

WHAT DO TEACHERS WANT FROM LEADERS?

One way to learn more about the whole teacher is to ask what they want from their school leader. At the start of a recent school year, prior to the upheavals caused by the COVID-19 pandemic, way before *remote learning* was a common term in K–12 schools, I asked the following question on Twitter and in our school:

"Teachers, if your principal did one thing for you to support you in the beginning of the school year, what would it be?"

Some of the responses I expected, but some were surprising. All the responses were insightful and have useful implications for school leaders.

As the dust settled from the whirlwind start to the new school year, I carved out some time to synthesize the responses. Five consistent themes quickly emerged. Across the country, teachers agreed that these five things would support them in doing their best work with students that school year.

Treat time like a precious commodity. The number one answer was time. Teachers are begging for meaningful meetings. They want their time with students to be top priority. They need time to prepare for the new school year, and they need adequate planning time throughout the year. They also want to take time to build relationships with students without feeling like they're falling behind on curriculum.

Show teachers they are valued. From little things like timely email replies and making sure information is double-checked for accuracy to big things like pointing out their strengths, teachers want to feel valued. They want to be trusted and know their leaders believe they are doing their best. Several teachers replied that they want their principals in their classrooms to check on them and offer a hand once in a while.

Ask questions. Using a Google Form, I sent out a one-question survey to the staff at our school. The survey was titled "Help Me Help You." The question was similar to the one I asked on Twitter: "What one thing could I do to support you right now?" The responses varied from "Teach me how to use my smart board" to "Help me understand how our new recess before lunch format will work." The most common response? "Thank you for asking." The Twitter responders concurred: teachers want their principals to ask them questions. They want to be asked how they're doing, what they need, what their goals are, and how their families are doing. The simple act of asking goes a long way.

Really listen. Another big theme in the responses was that teachers want their principals to really listen, to really hear them. They want principals to take a genuine interest in their lives. They want to share their hopes and dreams and fears. They'd like their leaders to take action based on their feedback, to create meaningful learning experiences for them. Teachers want principals to slow down, be in the moment with them, and put down their devices.

Show love for the kids and the work. Teachers work hard to get to know their students, and they want principals to do the same. There is nothing teachers enjoy more than watching their students soar, and they want to share that joy with their principals. When principals have fun and play with students, teachers feel like they have permission to do the same.

In addition to all we can learn from the teachers' responses, we can also learn from what they didn't say. As I combed through more than one hundred replies from teachers on Twitter and the input from the staff at my school, Quincy Elementary, there were only two responses that talked about food. That's not to say teachers don't appreciate chocolate and a catered meal once in a while, but what I learned here is that teachers care more about the five things above than they do about a taco bar. You will notice that there is little mention of food in the staff lounge in this book. Changing a school culture takes careful planning and it takes time, and leading the whole teacher calls for a deeper level of systematic change than typical teacher appreciation efforts. When we make piecemeal efforts to respond to teachers' concerns and stress levels, our responses are often surface level and disappear as soon as the school leader gets busy. Throughout this book, leaders will find strategies to support teachers right where they need it—and students will benefit, too.

WHAT CAN LEADERS DO FOR TEACHERS?

Let's dream for a moment about what school could be for teachers. How could we create a school environment that nurtures the whole teacher? What could a school set up for teacher success mean for students?

This book explores the six components of the whole teacher with strategies and ideas to make your school environment one that nurtures educators. When teachers are nurtured, they are better able to nurture their students. As shown in the following graphic, the six pillars we'll be discussing are:

- **Emotional safety.** Ensure emotional safety comes first by making school a safe space for teachers to have both successes and failures.
- **Valued educator.** Make sure teachers feel valued by recognizing their strengths.
- **Positive relationships.** Build healthy, strong, and positive relationships among all staff, students, and families.

- **Healthy workload.** Protect healthy workloads by removing responsibilities from teachers' plates when possible and encouraging them to hold family and personal time sacred.
- **Decision-maker.** Give teachers a seat at the decision-making table by empowering their voices.
- **Continuous learner.** Foster continuous growth and learning for teachers throughout the course of their careers.

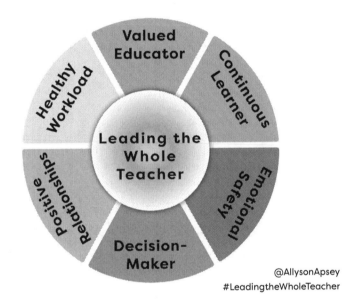

@AllysonApsey
#LeadingtheWholeTeacher

We'd like teachers to head home after a day of teaching feeling satisfied and fulfilled, and we want them to have a little energy left in their tank for their personal lives. We know this is good for teachers. We know this is good for students. It is good for teachers' families. We know it will positively impact the overall school environment. By implementing the strategies in this book and the ideas you come up with as you read, you can lead the whole teacher.

This book is designed to help readers reflect on strengths and strategies that are already in place in their schools and districts to support the whole teacher, but it's also meant to challenge readers to analyze where there are gaps. This book is full of strategies to help fill those gaps. If you're like me, you have sticky notes and a pen ready to go whenever you're reading a professional development book. You can use whatever note-taking strategy you'd like, but I invite you to begin by exploring the resources available to support this book. Visit AllysonApsey.com and find the Leading the Whole Teacher tab under the "Books" section. There you will find a note-taking guide that you can use as you read the book.

Onward and upward, my friends. We are in this together. As Ella Fitzgerald said, "It isn't where you came from. It's where you're going that counts." Wherever you're starting from as you create a school or district environment that supports the whole teacher, you are perfectly poised to take the first step—and then the next step. Slowly but surely, the culture will shift until teachers are running toward your school rather than running away from it.

Each chapter in this book ends with quick ideas that can be implemented tomorrow. Pick just one of the ideas to get started right away. Additionally, questions for collaboration and reflection are included to support book clubs and discussion with colleagues.

IDEAS TO IMPLEMENT TOMORROW:

- Reread the five things teachers say they want from their school leaders. Which of those are strengths of your leadership, and which are areas to focus on? How might you make a small adjustment to your practice tomorrow to start that improvement?

- If you're feeling very brave, send out an email to ask teachers what they're looking for in their leader given the current circumstances they're facing. Before you press Send, make sure you have your thick skin on because honest answers are key to trusting communication. Getting answers that sting a bit can be a good sign of honest dialogue.

- Visit AllysonApsey.com to begin exploring the free resources that accompany this book. Choose one resource to save to your computer or print to use as you read this book.

QUESTIONS FOR COLLABORATION AND REFLECTION:

- What surprised you about the data on the teacher shortage crisis?

- Which of the five things teachers want from leaders is an area of strength for you? What other ideas can you share?

- Looking at the six pillars of *Leading the Whole Teacher*, which might be an area of focus for you?

- Get connected with the #LeadingtheWholeTeacher community by sharing your ideas and connections on social media. Be sure to tag me (@AllysonApsey) and use #LeadingtheWholeTeacher.

CHAPTER 2

TAKING STOCK OF HOW TEACHERS ARE TREATED IN YOUR SCHOOL

It's not how much money we make that ultimately makes us happy between nine and five. It's whether or not our work fulfills us.

—Malcolm Gladwell

One of my favorite things to say to a teacher is this: "You are a person to me first, always." I say this when teachers share personal challenges, when they ask for career advice (even when that means leaving our school), or when they talk about balancing their workload. Wanting the best for teachers as people means wanting what's best for students. Fulfilled, satisfied, and passionate teachers set the foundation for engaged, excited, and high-achieving students.

A crucial first step in leading the whole teacher is to determine areas of strength and areas that need strengthening in your school culture. Dr. William Glasser's theory of five basic needs provides a powerful framework for this.[1] Dr. Glasser was a psychiatrist who developed the concepts of choice theory and reality therapy. I was fortunate to work in the first Glasser Quality School in the nation, Huntington

---

1 William Glasser, *Choice Theory* (New York: Harper Perennial, 1999).

Woods Elementary. Glasser Quality Schools base their school culture and philosophy on Dr. Glasser's work, notably focusing on meaningful learning experiences and strong, positive relationships free from extrinsic control. As a side note, I was also able to spend time with Dr. Glasser and his wife, Carleen, even taking him shopping for a necktie. Learning from Dr. Glasser is a highlight of my life in so many ways, and he influenced my work by helping me understand that all behavior is purposeful. He said that we all have five basic needs: love and belonging, freedom, power, fun, and survival. We are constantly trying to meet one or more of these five needs, and teachers need opportunities to meet them within the functions of their daily school life if school is going to be a nurturing environment.

I learned Glasser's choice theory during my first year of teaching, and I am not exaggerating when I say that it saved my career and made a huge impact on my personal life. In my first book, *The Path to Serendipity*, I wrote about how choice theory literally saved my marriage. I've spent many years studying choice theory and participating in Glasser's reality therapy, and his ideas are ingrained in me. Threads of choice theory and reality therapy run through our current work to create trauma-informed schools that implement restorative practices. In this chapter, I will use Glasser's choice theory as a tool to help you reflect on how to make school environments more nurturing for teachers.

In a nutshell, choice theory helps us understand the motivations behind behaviors. We learn that we have control over ourselves yet are unable to control others, and we discover how to develop and maintain strong, positive relationships. Reality therapy is a process to help someone evaluate their choices so they can move toward a more effective life. The five basic needs help us understand why we make the choices we do and how we can shift our choices to more effective ones when necessary.[2]

---

2 Glasser, *Choice Theory*.

When learning any new concept, it helps to apply it to yourself first to develop understanding. We will do that with Glasser's five basic needs as they pertain to your teachers and your school. But wait! Before you continue reading, please get out a piece of paper and a pen so you can take notes as I ask you questions throughout this chapter.

Divide your paper into two columns and five rows. Label the two columns "Already in Place" and "Next Steps." Label each row with one of the five basic needs: love and belonging, freedom, power, fun, and survival. If you prefer, you can visit AllysonApsey.com and look for the Leading the Whole Teacher tab under the "Books" section to find resources and download a note-taking chart. If you're not yet sure what to include as "Next Steps," don't worry one little bit. This entire book is full of ideas to help you with those. I've got you!

As you fill out this chart, remember that it's important to focus on the need-satisfying elements already in place at your school as you think through the elements that aren't in place yet. We can get overwhelmed and discouraged when we only focus on the "need to do" and forget about all the great things we already have done!

An additional note before we dive into the five basic needs: the only person who can meet your needs is you. We cannot meet the five basic needs of others, but we can create environments that support people in meeting their own needs. As we think through the five basic needs, please keep this in mind.

LOVE AND BELONGING

According to Glasser, we are born with needs of varying strengths. Some of us need more of a particular need than others.[3] For example, I have a huge need for love and belonging. It helps to think of each need as a gas tank. My gas tank for belonging is big, and it's important to me to have lots of interpersonal connections throughout the day. Since I spend my days in schools full of people, that is pretty easy for me to

---

3 Glasser, *Choice Theory.*

accomplish. However, what about teachers who are new to the school and don't know many people yet? What about teachers who aren't comfortable initiating conversations with colleagues? What about teachers who feel overwhelmed by their workload and feel like they need to spend every minute of their school day grading papers or making lesson plans? How can we support these teachers in meeting their need for belonging at school?

How do you meet *your* need for belonging during the school day? Do you visit the lunchroom to see other staff members? Do you go to recess with students? Do you take a few minutes at the beginning of the day to walk around and check in on people? How do you connect with others to meet your need to feel loved and to belong?

You may already have systems in place to give teachers opportunities to connect with each other throughout the school day or the week. If you don't, this might be an area of focus for you.

FREEDOM

It is often tricky for teachers to meet their need for freedom during the school day. They hardly have time to go to the bathroom, much less do anything that isn't an expected part of their responsibilities. How do you meet *your* need for freedom during the school day? For example, do you take a break to breathe or to read an article? When I was a teacher, I would leave my coat hanging on the back of my chair rather than hang it up in the closet. It served as a reminder that I would have some freedom at the end of the day. Does your school have systems in place to help teachers meet their need for freedom during the school day? Or might they stare longingly at their coats, waiting anxiously for freedom?

Giving teachers freedom to use the bathroom, allowing them to let go of some responsibilities occasionally, and providing them some independence supports them in meeting their need for freedom throughout the school day. It gives them choice.

POWER

The need for power gets a bad reputation, but it doesn't need to be power over others. Instead, our power need can be met through our successes, being asked to share our ideas, or empowering others. Teachers and principals often have opportunities to meet their need for power throughout the day as they lead students. Dr. Martin Luther King Jr. defined it like this: "Power properly understood is nothing but the ability to achieve purpose."

Sometimes our need for power takes a hit, such as when decisions are made for us without our input or when we are not able to achieve our purpose. For instance, a teacher may have an incredible lesson planned to help students learn a complicated concept, but that lesson might be interrupted by a child in crisis, an unexpected fire drill, or any number of things.

When do *you* feel powerful at school? Conversely, what interferes with meeting your power need? How might teachers at your school meet their need for power? Do you have a system in place that allows teachers to meet this need? Do you have a way to address frequent interruptions that are preventing them from achieving their purpose?

FUN

I remember an aha moment midway through the 2020–2021 school year. Deep in the trenches of COVID-19 prevention protocols, we had to navigate abrupt changes to those safety protocols weekly, if not daily. It felt like I was treading water to keep my head up, and this was in my eighteenth year as a principal!

While I don't remember exactly what prompted my aha moment, I do remember feeling like I wanted to smack myself upside the head for neglecting fun and play. Amid the struggle of leading a school during a crisis, I had forgotten that fun was a need, not just a want. Before the pandemic, I had walked the halls wearing my fanny pack with speakers to play music during arrival, dismissal, and recess. So I got my fanny pack back out, and I also started dressing up in costume again. We brought play back into our school. And you know what? Teachers and students (and likely families) gave a collective sigh of relief. At last, one thing felt right and normal again.

Want some great news? According to Dr. Glasser, the act of learning—real, deep, authentic learning—can help staff and students meet their needs for fun and power.[4] We know that fun is often the first thing to go when we are in panic or crisis mode. Yet this is exactly when we need to lighten the situation a bit. We need opportunities to play and have fun. And as leaders, the invitation to include fun starts with us.

Think through how fun is incorporated into daily life in your school. Are there systems or routines that make fun commonplace? Or is it the first thing to fly out the window when times get tough?

SURVIVAL

Our need to survive encompasses the physical aspects of our survival—food, shelter, and water—as well as the psychological components, such as our need to feel safe, secure, and free from threat in our environment. For our staff and students who have strong relationships and relatively healthy home lives, creating a school environment that meets these needs is pretty simple: we prioritize needs such as eating and staying hydrated and focus on encouraging strong, positive relationships. But for our staff and students who have experienced trauma without being nurtured, it is a different story. It requires more concerted effort to meet their need to feel safe in the school environment. The next chapter dives into ways to make our schools emotionally safe environments for our teachers. This is the first pillar of the book because without emotional safety for our teachers in schools, the other pillars cannot exist.

---

4 William Glasser, *The Quality School: Managing Students without Coercion*, 3rd ed. (New York: Harper Perennial, 1998).

How does your school help your staff and students meet their physical need to survive? For example, is staff lunchtime held sacred? Can teachers call the office for a quick tap-out to take care of a physical need like using the bathroom? Also, how does your school meet the psychological components of surviving? Does it help well-regulated teachers and students feel emotionally safe at school? What extra support is provided for dysregulated staff and students?

Whew! That was a lot of reflecting. Way to go—you should be proud of all the "Already in Place" items you listed. As you look through your "Next Steps" column, take a few moments to circle priorities. Thinking through the unique needs of the staff in your school, where does it make the most sense to begin? Sometimes thinking about making a lot of changes can be overwhelming, so check below for quick changes you can implement tomorrow to help you in your journey to leading the whole teacher.

IDEAS TO IMPLEMENT TOMORROW:

- Take stock of Glasser's needs for yourself. Using the questions in this chapter, rank the strength of each need for yourself on a scale of one to five. Do this before asking your teachers to do the same in the next activity. (Visit AllysonApsey.com for a worksheet to guide you in this.)

- Consider teaching your staff about the five basic needs during one of your upcoming staff meetings. If you are not ready to schedule this right away, set a reminder on your calendar to revisit this idea. During the meeting, give them an opportunity to rank the strength of their own needs on a scale of one to five. Then guide them in an activity where they identify ways they can meet their needs in the current school environment. Help them identify any gaps, and then collectively use this information to develop next steps in creating a need-satisfying school.

- Look back over the notes you took during this chapter and the priorities you circled in your notes. Which one can you start working on tomorrow? Create a timeline and a plan for when you want to implement the other changes.

- As you look through your own daily school schedule, identify things that will be fun for you. It's important that leaders model fun for teachers and students. Make sure you have at least one opportunity for fun and play every day—and not just with students. Have fun and play with teachers and colleagues, too. Could you greet them with music when they walk in the door tomorrow? Could you put a silly trivia question up on the board in the staff lounge? How about heading out to recess and racing students? Or swinging high with them on the playground? You could have students pick their favorite books to read to you. Whatever sounds the most fun to you, do it!

QUESTIONS FOR COLLABORATION AND REFLECTION:

- After thinking through how to meet your own needs each day, what changes are you considering that would make school a more need-satisfying place for you?

- What need do teachers in your school have the hardest time meeting? Share ideas to support teachers in meeting that need.

- Don't forget to share your great ideas with the #LeadingtheWholeTeacher community on social media.

CHAPTER 3

ENSURING THAT EMOTIONAL SAFETY COMES FIRST

Tenderness and kindness are not signs of weakness and despair, but manifestations of strength and resolution.

—Kahlil Gibran

Active shooter drills, student behavior challenges, ever-increasing curricular demands, evaluations based on single-shot, high-stakes testing: any and all of these could make a teacher feel physically or emotionally unsafe at school—or both. As I travel the country conducting workshops, I ask participants: "What might make a teacher feel unsafe at school?" Inevitably, their answers include things on this list.

However, again and again, the answers that rise to the top are interpersonal issues with colleagues or administrators, such as gossip and judgment. It is especially powerful to create a word cloud from the responses; when a response is entered multiple times by various participants, the word gets larger. This compelling graphic gives us keen insight into what makes teachers feel unsafe at school, and a surprising number of these issues are within our control.

In this example, thirty-eight teachers from a rural midwestern school district answered the question. As you can see in in the graphic, some responses are specific to their region. For example, mud poses a safety concern in this area because heavy rainfall results in muddy and hazardous roads. According to this group of teachers, even more threatening than mud, blizzards, or weapons is gossip in the workplace.

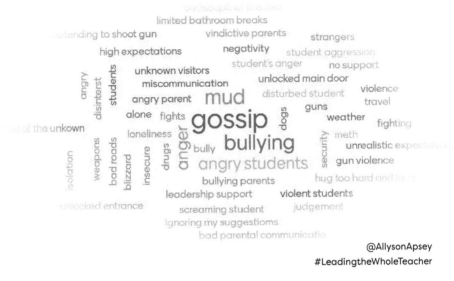

@AllysonApsey
#LeadingtheWholeTeacher

Many things are beyond the control of teachers and administrators, but creating an environment free of toxic behaviors like gossip is not one of them. Every teacher deserves to walk into school knowing they are supported by colleagues and leaders, and every teacher deserves to feel like part of an interdependent team. It takes constant and deliberate effort to fight against our human instincts of defensiveness and fear, and in this chapter we will explore strategies to create a school environment that is psychologically safe for teachers.

In *Help for Billy: A Beyond Consequences Approach to Helping Challenging Children in the Classroom*, Heather T. Forbes's book on trauma-informed practices for students, Forbes describes the concept of a window of stress tolerance.[1] In short, everyone has a baseline of

---

1 Heather T. Forbes, *Help for Billy: A Beyond Consequences Approach to Helping Challenging Children in the Classroom* (Boulder, CO: Beyond Consequences Institute, 2012), 19.

stress, and for some that baseline almost fills their window of stress tolerance. As shown in the graphic, baseline stressors for teachers include getting through all the content, making sure students develop mastery, managing student behavior, and squeezing every last minute out of the day to fit everything in. In addition, some teachers need to manage students who struggle with regulating their behavior, disrupt the learning of the entire classroom, and may even act violently.

We all have stressors in our personal lives as well. It's easy to imagine that many teachers have small windows of stress tolerance, which means, as Forbes describes in *Help for Billy*, many teachers may live only moments away from their breaking point.[2] Helping teachers reduce their baseline stress will enable them to enlarge their windows of stress tolerance. As a result, they will feel more emotionally safe at school and better able to manage the additional stressors that pop up during the day.

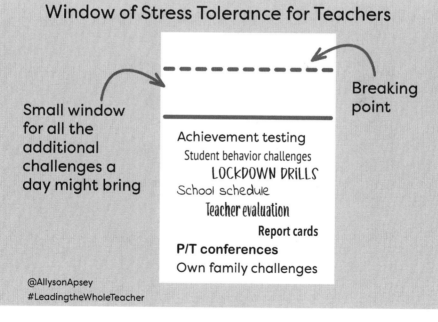

Window of Stress Tolerance for Teachers

Small window for all the additional challenges a day might bring

Breaking point

Achievement testing
Student behavior challenges
LOCKDOWN DRILLS
School schedule
Teacher evaluation
Report cards
P/T conferences
Own family challenges

@AllysonApsey
#LeadingtheWholeTeacher

---

2 Forbes, *Help for Billy*, 139.

As Forbes notes, reducing baseline stress increases patience, emotional regulation, and flexibility[3]—three crucial and valuable traits for educators. Principals play an important part in helping teachers reduce baseline stress, as do colleagues. Self-care is also instrumental in reducing stress, and for self-care to exist at school as a regular practice, we need to work in emotionally safe environments. (Strategies for personal wellness are included in chapters 6 and 9.) We all have an opportunity to help each other feel emotionally safe at school, and we all have an obligation to make sure we are not causing stress for each other.

THE PRINCIPAL'S ROLE IN CREATING AN EMOTIONALLY SAFE ENVIRONMENT

I was speaking to a group of over two hundred Michigan principals the first time I asked, "What might make a teacher feel unsafe at school?" I had no idea what their responses would be, and I was absolutely shocked to see the results. Take a look for yourself at the graphic below.

@AllysonApsey
#LeadingtheWholeTeacher

---

3 Forbes, *Help for Billy*, 140–142.

I could not believe the top answer among the principals was that evaluation was the leading cause of teachers feeling unsafe at school; we will dive deeper into that topic in the next chapter. Notice that the word *bully* looms large in the word cloud. This group of principals also listed bullying as a reason teachers don't feel safe at school.

In talking with the principals, I discovered they were not thinking of children being bullied; they were thinking of their colleagues. Bullying among teachers is a major concern at many schools, and it is a result of toxic environments full of fear. Teachers bully for the same reason children bully: they feel powerless and weak and are attempting to strengthen themselves by bringing others down. School leaders are obligated to not only address bullying behavior among staff but to also prevent it by creating a need-satisfying, healthy school environment.

The first step in creating a healthy school environment is to model the behavior that leads to a supportive and loving staff. The modeling starts at the top, with the principal. Just like teachers cannot expect students to treat each other with care when they do not model that same behavior toward students, principals cannot expect teachers to treat each other with consideration and kindness if they do not lead with compassion and grace.

The importance of clear and thorough communication and its close tie with an emotionally safe environment is often overlooked. As George Bernard Shaw said so well, "The single biggest problem in communication is the illusion that it has taken place." Here are five communication tips that will help staff feel well informed, listened to, and secure.

Say what you mean and mean what you say.

Teachers want honest leaders who follow through on what they say. A trusting environment is foundational to an emotionally safe environment, and honest communication must begin with school leaders. Teachers also want transparent communicators, because the source of many conflicts between colleagues or between principals and teachers is misunderstanding or assumptions caused by a lack of communication. If you don't really mean it, don't say it. If you do mean it and are willing to follow through, say it over and over in a variety of ways so it will be understood by all.

Don't ask questions unless you want the answers.

When describing frustrations at school, teachers often share that they get frustrated when they feel like they don't have a voice at the decision-making table. This frustration is made worse when they're asked to share their thoughts and then feel like their input is disregarded. To prevent such an erosion of trust, school leaders need to actively seek out teacher input on decisions and also make sure they don't ask questions unless they really want the answers. The concept of generating buy-in from teachers is antiquated. For teachers to thrive and feel emotionally safe at school, they need to participate in every step of the decision-making process. Whether they are making the decisions, influencing the decisions, or providing implementation input, teachers give valuable insight that can contribute to a well-thought-out plan that feels right to everyone.

Once you ask a question, it's time to listen carefully.

Really listening requires an open mind. Ironically, having an open mind begins with acknowledging our own biases, and it often helps to reveal our biases to each other. For example, when I discuss class management strategies with a teacher, I share that my training is in William Glasser's choice theory, which greatly influences my thoughts on classroom management. Recognizing that I have strong opinions on classroom management and that my responses will be biased by them is honest, and it is helpful modeling. We all have biases, and not all of them are bad; sharing them with each other builds trust. Teachers confide their concerns to leaders they trust. All it takes is asking the questions, carefully listening to the responses, and then taking action based on staff input.

Ask teachers in your school what makes them feel unsafe.

Creating a word cloud with a tool like Mentimeter is a compelling way to share teacher responses. When it's finished, look at the responses together and ask these questions: "Which of these do we have direct control over? Which can we influence? Which do we have no control over?" These questions can guide small groups of teachers to brainstorm strategies to help all teachers feel safe at school. This powerful information can help them better support each other, and school leaders can use the information to guide school-wide initiatives.

Confront problem behavior like staff gossip and bullying with compassion and honesty.

Teachers trust leaders who are not afraid to have difficult and crucial conversations that result in change. So often people simply are not aware of the negative impact of their behavior, and helping a staff member become aware of it is the first step. Withholding judgment is important when beginning a difficult conversation, and we can do that by leading with curiosity. Try opening with questions like these: "Could you tell me a little more about [issue]?" or "I am wondering how you're feeling about [issue]?" This allows the staff member to share first, which is both empowering for them and enlightening for the principal. Often the teacher is concerned about the exact same issue I am, and that common ground gives us a great launchpad for a plan for change. If the teacher is not at all concerned about the issue, that is important information that can inform the rest of the conversation. Confronting problems head on does not have to be confrontational; instead, it can be compassionate yet still lead to change without damaging relationships or trust.

COLLEAGUES' ROLE IN CREATING AN EMOTIONALLY SAFE ENVIRONMENT

In my nearly twenty-five years in education, I have never met a teacher who wanted bad things for their colleagues. Instead, I have met dozens of teachers who would bend over backward to help a struggling colleague. The challenge is that teachers don't feel equipped with the skills and strategies to support their colleagues through the myriad challenges they face.

During a conversation about why teaching seems so much harder than it used to be, a teacher I was speaking with remarked that although we have always had students with behavior difficulties, it seemed easier to help them before. She wondered why and came up with two reasons that really stuck with her: First, teachers face so many more demands because of the fast pace of the curriculum and high-stakes tests. Second, so many more students have behavior difficulties.

Teachers work hard to create meaningful research-informed and curriculum-aligned lesson plans, build in empowering and engaging activities for students, and continually monitor their progress—and that's just a fraction of what teachers need to do every day. Some teachers can walk into their classrooms in the morning knowing their day will unfold as planned. Some walk into their classrooms prepared and flexible yet cross their fingers that their day won't be derailed by a student with a behavior escalation. Some teachers don't know if they will be teaching in their classroom or in the library; it will depend on the kind of day their student in crisis is having. And some go home with papers to grade *and* bruises on their leg because an escalated student kicked them.

In any given school, one or two students could have a behavior crisis at any given moment—or there may be dozens of students who could escalate. When a colleague faces this type of challenge, our hearts break and we want to fix it for them. But what do our colleagues really need from us? How can we support them so they feel strong and confident enough to take on this challenge without feeling drained and insecure? We know that nurturing, supportive adults can serve as a buffer and lessen the impact of trauma for children. Could the same be true for colleagues? Could a nurturing, supportive colleague serve as a trauma buffer for a teacher?

Let's hold a mirror to ourselves for a moment. When you face an overwhelming challenge and doubt your handling of it because it doesn't seem to be getting any better, who do you turn to for support? Sometimes it's the person in closest proximity, but when you really think it through, who is it? What makes that person so comforting and supportive? When I think about this, I think of someone who knows my values and who I really am. I think of someone who validates my feelings, empathizes rather than sympathizes with me, and helps me keep the size of the problem in check. I also value people who help me separate my emotions from the actual problem. Sometimes I am too emotional to talk the situation over with anyone, but when I am ready to talk about it, I look for someone who does the following four things.

Validate feelings.

When we are struggling, we look for people who help us normalize our feelings. When someone reaches out to you, it is important to listen to understand instead of listening to respond or to solve the problem. Ask questions and paraphrase what they say to make sure you are accurately hearing them and so your colleague knows they are truly being listened to.

Empathize.

There are major differences between commiserating and empathizing, and it can be difficult to know what to say to a colleague who needs to vent about a problem. As Brené Brown says, we don't want to "silver lining" the problem by saying things like "Well, at least you have a job, right?"[4] That can feel like we are minimizing a problem that feels big to our colleague.

Empathy is feeling *with* the person. It is not putting yourself in their shoes because it doesn't matter how *you* would feel in the situation. What matters is how your colleague feels right then, at that moment. Empathetic responses often include questions like "How can I help you right now?" Sometimes our colleagues will ask us to just listen, or they might say they don't know how we can help. We can offer options by asking if they want us just to listen or to problem solve. Throwing in some humor usually helps, too—taking a break from the big negative feelings with a belly laugh can spark hope and creativity.

Keep the problem as small as possible.

Sometimes we think empathizing sounds like this: "Yes, students these days are so different and so difficult. I don't know how they expect us to teach and handle these students." Or we might think empathizing sounds like this: "Yes, you have one of the worst classes I've ever seen. I don't know how you do it." Sound familiar? We say these things with the best intentions, but they do not help us keep the problem as small and manageable as possible. They make the problem huge, and there is no way we can fix "students these days" or "the worst class I have ever seen." Instead, let's help our colleagues focus on the main problem with questions like this: "If you could fix just one specific thing right now, what would that be?" If they need time to think that question over, give them time and circle back later in the day or the next day.

Separate emotions from the problem.

It's helpful to think of problems in two parts: how we feel about the problem and what the problem actually is. They really are separate yet intimately connected problems. When I talk with someone who helps

---

4 Brené Brown, "The Power of Vulnerability," filmed June 2010 at TEDxHouston, Houston, TX, TED video, 20:03, ted.com/talks/brene_brown_the_power_of _vulnerability.

me take my emotions out of the problem, it literally cuts the problem in half. When we support a student in crisis, deal with an angry parent, or confront any other emotionally charged problem, we feel overwhelmed, insecure, and vulnerable. But the actual problem is usually not about us at all. Layering our emotions on top of the problem is normal, but it's helpful to recognize we're doing this so we can work to solve the problem as two separate issues.

These four tips help us support colleagues in most instances, but when in doubt, when you have no idea how to help, try a random act of kindness. It *always* helps. Set a flower on a colleague's desk, surprise them with a cold Diet Coke, text them the silliest joke you can find, or write them a little note of encouragement. Those simple acts can make someone's load feel a million times lighter.

COLLABORATION WITHOUT COMPETITION

When we consider supporting our colleagues, there are a couple of don'ts to keep in mind: don't judge and don't compete. No colleague wants a kick of judgment when they're facing challenges and plagued with self-doubt. Teaching is not a competitive sport, and safe environments are free from both judgment and unhealthy competition. When we have a team of people behind us, we feel like we can slay any challenge that comes our way. When we feel judgmental eyes evaluating our every move, even the simplest challenge can feel overwhelming. In fact, numerous studies have identified that collective teacher efficacy is the number one influence on student achievement.

This is more than just teachers believing they have what it takes to help students succeed. John Hattie, world-renowned educational researcher, professor of education, and director of the Melbourne Education Research Institute at the University of Melbourne, Australia, defines collective teacher efficacy this way: "Collective Teacher Efficacy is the collective belief of teachers in their ability to positively affect students."[5]

When considering the importance of creating an environment full of teacher collaboration and free from unhealthy competition, Hattie's phrase "positively affect students" stands out. When we work together to help students succeed, the sky is the limit. We need each other to succeed so we can succeed ourselves. Students win when teachers recognize that there is enough success to go around, and when we share our successes, we are all better for it.

THE ROLE OF SELF-CARE IN CREATING AN EMOTIONALLY SAFE ENVIRONMENT

Emotional safety begins within because often the voices in our own heads are our biggest critics. We are all human and beautifully flawed. Seeking a perfection that doesn't even exist can do more damage than a bullying colleague ever could. Accepting our own humanness and becoming more self-aware is the first step to creating emotional safety.

Leah Kuypers is an education leader who created the Zones of Regulation, a great tool to support self-awareness.[6] The four zones help us identify how we feel, understand our behavior, and implement strategies to get back into the green zone, where we are in most effective control. This tool is used widely in schools to teach self-awareness and self-regulation to students. When we first adopted it at our school, it positively impacted adults as much as or more than it impacted our students.

The zones represent our energy level, with blue being our lowest energy level and red being our highest. There are people in our lives

---

5 "Collective Teacher Efficacy (CTE) according to John Hattie," accessed August 10, 2022, Visible Learning, visible-learning.org/2018/03/collective-teacher-efficacy -hattie/.

6 Leah Kuypers, *The Zones of Regulation* (Think Social Publishing, Inc., 2011), socialthinking.com.

who are excited and full of energy who positively live in the red zone, and we wouldn't want them any other way. The green zone is typically the ideal state for learning. Pausing and identifying which zone we're in can help us determine if we're at the appropriate energy level for what we want to accomplish. For instance, if I'm about to have a crucial conversation with a staff member, I definitely don't want to be in the red zone. I will want to utilize strategies to make sure I am in the green zone for the conversation—or minimally in the yellow zone.

When we identify ourselves as having negative emotions in the yellow or red zone, we know our judgment may be impacted by how we feel, so before making any decisions, we may want to try a calming strategy like drinking a glass of water or taking a few deep breaths. When we're in the blue zone, we know that how we feel physically may take a toll on our patience, and an energizing strategy like brisk physical exercise may be helpful.

We visit all the zones from time to time, and that is perfectly OK. Living most of our lives in the green zone rather than in the blue zone is hugely dependent on how we take care of ourselves physically. We cannot underestimate the impact on our emotional regulation of getting a good night's sleep, eating right, and exercising. Consistent nighttime and morning routines can help us with our sleep habits and set us up for success. Taking care of ourselves must be our highest priority if we want to do our best work with students and be supportive of our colleagues.

STUDENTS WIN WHEN TEACHERS FEEL EMOTIONALLY SAFE AT SCHOOL

When teachers do not feel emotionally safe at school, they are full of fear. Fear leads to self-doubt, mistrust, and lack of communication. When teachers feel valued and safe to freely share their ideas and celebrate colleagues, the sky's the limit, and their impact on students is tremendous. Teachers who feel safe have the mental stamina to get creative, and they have the resilience to work through any challenges that come their way. Feeling safe opens the door to feeling happy at school, and we all know that happy teachers lead to happy students just as unhappy teachers lead to unhappy students. Leading the whole teacher means creating an environment where teachers feel emotionally safe at school, which is a win not only for teachers but for their students as well.

IDEAS TO IMPLEMENT TOMORROW:

- Ask teachers what makes them feel unsafe at school. Use a tool like Mentimeter's Word Cloud to create a graphic with their responses. Then work in small teams to identify what things you have direct control over. Mix the teams up so they can share the ideas from their previous discussions and come up with action steps to address the concerns.
- Use the window of stress tolerance concept to help identify the stressors teachers face daily. See if there is one stressor you can help reduce or eliminate so that teachers can reduce their baseline stress.
- Use the Zones of Regulation to help increase your own awareness of what zone you're in throughout the day. Identify which strategies help you get back into the green zone. This personal application may lead you to teach staff about the Zones of Regulation so they can identify their feelings, regulate their emotions, and communicate their feelings with colleagues.
- Visit AllysonApsey.com for a printable PDF of the four ways colleagues can help create an emotionally safe environment for each other.
- Share your brilliant ideas and the connections you made to this chapter using #LeadingtheWholeTeacher.

QUESTIONS FOR COLLABORATION AND REFLECTION:

- Did anything surprise you about teachers' responses when they were asked what makes them feel unsafe at school?

- What might be filling teachers' window of stress tolerance in your school? What is one thing you might do to reduce baseline stress for them?

- What is one thing you could do to help colleagues better support each other in your school?

CHAPTER 4

HELPING TEACHERS
FEEL VALUED

To feel valued, to know, if even only once in a while, that you can do a job well is an absolutely marvelous feeling.

—Barbara Walters

Do teachers at your school know there is no place you would rather be than in their classrooms watching them teach? Helping teachers feel valued is a daily job, not something reserved for Teacher Appreciation Day, and they don't know that your favorite spot in the school is their classroom unless you tell them and show them.

Over-the-top celebrations are fun and contribute to a culture of gratitude for teachers' hard work, and the second section of this chapter will focus on celebrating teachers all year. But the first section of this chapter will focus on the most important thing: working hard alongside teachers to empower them in their work.

I'd like to share a story that embarrasses me greatly. Let me give you a bit of context first. My first teaching position was in an elementary school in our hometown. My husband and I had been married just a few months, and we dreamed of moving away to forge a life on our own (ah, young dreamers!). The problem was that I really loved my school and was deeply influenced by its unique philosophy. As I mentioned in chapter 2, we were a Glasser Quality School, which had team-taught, multiage classrooms and an extended school year, and we were project based back when we called it *meaningful thematic instruction.*

Well, serendipity happened in that the former principal of my school opened a new school in Traverse City, Michigan, a couple of hours north of where we lived. This school would have a similar philosophy, so I asked her for a job. She said yes, and we moved. Because I was the only teacher experienced in the unique philosophy of the school, I quickly became a teacher leader, and within a few years I became one of the school's principals. It was a different kind of principalship because my boss, the superintendent, worked alongside me all day, every day, coaching me. As with anything, there were great blessings in that situation and great challenges. I learned so much, but I also had little freedom to do things my way.

For reasons that could fill another book, I left that principalship after fourteen years, and we moved our family back near our hometown. I accepted the principal position at Quincy Elementary in Zeeland, Michigan, and I reveled in the independence I found in leading according to my own values and philosophy. I say all this because I hope with all my heart that the embarrassing story I am about to tell you would never happen at Quincy Elementary.

I can try to blame someone else for what I did, but ultimately, regardless of the reason, I used that awful, inactionable, judgmental word: *lackadaisical.* And it had devastating consequences that I didn't even realize until about three years into my new position in Zeeland when I received this message from a teacher I had worked with in Traverse City:

Hello Allyson! Congrats on your job downstate and your debut to FB Live. I just finished watching a good portion of it. You were my favorite of all 3 principals years ago at GTA.

Who I saw in the video tonight was the you I remembered and liked. However, there was one time that completely crushed me as a teacher. You came into my classroom for 5 minutes, wrote a review and called my teaching "lackadaisical." That was one of the worst words I felt used to describe my teaching. That was truly the icing on the cake as to why I left the school—fortunately that was the only negative encounter we had during my 4 years there. I always enjoyed seeing your enthusiasm. Your videos are even more enjoyable. I honestly have not looked back and thought much about my days at our school until I got a friend request from you. Ironically, it did help me put your review in perspective. On a scale of enthusiasm you are a 10. I am about a 6. That is all it was. It was a completely controlled classroom of quiet workers in math who didn't need flashy songs and lights that day. It was just a matter of a 5 minute snapshot into my day. I honestly write this not to hurt you. Honestly. I write this to say how proud I am of you for growing over the years and hearing you say how you need to take care of your students and staff. I don't know what it's like in your school, but I can pretty well guess that you do your very best to walk in a room and assess and ask questions before making a judgment, both of students and staff. There probably was not a super-classy way to send this message, but I hope you understand. You never know how far words will carry with a child/teacher . . . it sounds like you are making wonderful strides. Keep up the good work!

Ouch. That message hurt because it is exactly the opposite of the leader I hope I am today. And I almost can't believe I am sharing it with you, because I am still so embarrassed. Initially I felt defensive and wasn't sure how to respond. Eventually I worked through my feelings of shame enough to craft a response, and here is what it said:

Hi [name], I appreciate you reaching out. I hope you are doing well. I definitely do understand how far words carry, and how hurtful words (or even a word) can be. I am so far from perfect and definitely have made and will continue to make mistakes, hopefully not ones as hurtful as that mistake was to you. I am so sorry to have hurt you and it hurts my heart that a comment I made was the icing on the cake for you leaving the school. I assure you that I aspire to be a better person each day and hope that the many days between then and now, I am the support person that my teachers need me to be. I have written a lot about mistakes I have made and what I have learned from them on my blog. Here is a link to one that relates to the comment I made to you [link to blog post titled "Strengths-Based Feedback"]. Maybe this will help you see how much I have learned since then. Best wishes to you and your family. Thank you for reaching out!

When I read over my response to her, there are so many other things I wish I had said. I wish I had told her how I remember the way her gentle and genuine smile could light up a room. I wish I had made my response less about me and more about her. But I will not edit the past; I will learn from it.

I felt an incredible sense of relief when I got her generous response:

Thank you for taking the time to respond. What a beautiful blog. I love that you took the time to write this piece. I wish many more admins would look at this approach. It's pretty incredible to see how staff and principals interact and how much joy they find in their jobs when building one another up in true love and care for each other. You needn't have apologized. But I appreciate that. Thank you. And the "icing on the cake" was probably one of the sweetest icings LOL. I believe there are no accidents in life and God placed me in that school so I could be where I am today. Keep on doing what you're doing. Your smile is contagious and you are obviously a very thoughtful and reflective person who continues to grow. I wish you well!

I am writing about these messages years later (with the permission of the teacher), so it obviously stuck with me. Feedback that stings badly usually does, and in this case I am extremely grateful. I never want to make a teacher feel that way again, and here are three tips I try to live by to support this effort.

Don't give inactionable judgment.

This teacher's message illustrates the damage that can be done when we give teachers inactionable judgment disguised as feedback. (Sidenote: I don't think *inactionable* is actually a word, but we are going to make it a word and define it as "unable to take action." Let's chalk it up to artistic freedom.) What was I thinking using a word like *lackadaisical*? What could the teacher do with that information other than crawl into a hole and cry? Our teachers deserve actionable feedback that they can do something with, preferably something that empowers them to feel better about their next steps.

Instead, ask questions.

Instead, I could have asked the teacher, "How do you think students were feeling during the lesson? How could you tell? If you could change one thing to engage students differently, what would it be?" With guiding questions, most teachers easily reflect on what went well and what didn't in a lesson. And they are usually harder on themselves than we ever could be. Our job is to help them think in a different way that will help them get better results and then to provide whatever support they need to turn their thinking into action. They don't need our judgment; they need our guidance and expertise.

Don't play the "guess what I am thinking" game.

A former boss would ask me tough questions—but not because she wanted my answers. She wanted me to guess what her answer was. Rather than activating my own creative thinking and moving me forward, guessing her answer made me nervous. Instead of being reflective, I was focused on being right. This frustrated me because I knew she was not interested in my thinking. I bumbled and got defensive, and eventually I gave up and just played the game. If we are going to ask questions, it is important that we are open to other ways of thinking than our own.

EVALUATION AS A TEACHER EMPOWERMENT TOOL

In *Dare to Lead*, Brené Brown writes, "Daring leaders sit down with their team members and have real rumbles with them about the contributions they make so that everyone knows where they're strong. Once everyone understands their value, we stop hustling for worthiness and we lean into our gifts."[1]

What if our sole purpose for teacher evaluation was to help teachers lean into their gifts?

Let's take another look at the word cloud that was created by over two hundred Michigan principals. This time, let's focus on the biggest word right in the middle: *evaluation*. As I mentioned in chapter 3, this was truly one of the most profound moments I've ever had when leading a workshop.

Evaluation? I couldn't believe my eyes. This group of principals thought teacher evaluation was the biggest cause of teachers feeling unsafe at school. Over school violence? Over interpersonal conflicts with colleagues? Over aggressive students? I was shocked because in Michigan, where I was a school leader, we have lots of flexibility in how

---

1 Brené Brown, *Dare to Lead: Brave Work. Tough Conversations. Whole Hearts.* (New York: Random House, 2018), 98.

we implement the teacher evaluation process, which, in my mind, lends itself to utilizing the system to coach and empower teachers.

@AllysonApsey
#LeadingtheWholeTeacher

Now that I have asked this question over and over, I am no longer surprised by this response. I have heard from both principals and teachers across the country that evaluation is a feared practice with few benefits for anyone. Teacher evaluation may be directed by state policies, but how it *feels* to teachers is not part of the state's directives. Instead, how evaluation feels to a teacher is determined by the evaluator. Does it empower teachers and push them to continuously improve? Is it focused on their strengths? Do they feel like it's their principal's favorite thing to do because they love to watch teachers work their magic in the classroom? The principals who called evaluation the leading cause of teachers feeling unsafe at school may not think the answer to any of these questions is yes. But the answer to these questions absolutely *could* be yes, and helping teachers feel valued and empowered as a result of evaluation would contribute to an emotionally safe school environment for them.

Let's liken teacher evaluation to student grades in the classroom. If we asked a group of teachers what might make students feel unsafe at school, what would we say if grades was the number one answer? Principals might respond with something like this: "Really? With all the challenges our students face with each other, their home lives, and their own development, grades are the scariest thing? Don't teachers have control over how grades feel to our students?" Yes they do. Just like principals have control over how evaluation feels to teachers.

Research helps us recognize that there is little correlation between teacher evaluation systems and student achievement. When looking at John Hattie's research, we see that practices such as collective teacher efficacy, self-reported grades, and response to intervention have big effect sizes and can significantly improve student achievement. In fact, Hattie's research shows that collective teacher efficacy has a bigger positive impact on student achievement than any other educational practice he researched.[2] Effect size is commonly used in research to figure out the relationship between two things; in this case, we are looking at the relationship between specific school interventions/influences and student achievement.

However, teacher evaluation systems often fail to focus on the things that have the biggest impact on learning, and they don't take into consideration that many of the practices that most impact learning are systemic and not solely dependent on individual teacher's performance. The bottom line? Teacher evaluation systems do not work to increase student achievement. But we can use required teacher evaluation systems to coach and empower teachers, which will contribute to teacher job satisfaction and professional growth. When we use evaluation to help teachers see their value, they feel strong, positive, and good about their contribution—and they are ready to learn and grow. When teachers seek continuous improvement, it positively impacts student achievement. Here are some tips for evaluation.

---

2 John Hattie, *Visible Learning: A Synthesis of Over 800 Meta-Analyses Relating to Achievement* (London: Routledge, 2008).

Prioritize the feedback meeting.

In *Leverage Leadership: A Practical Guide to Building Exceptional Schools*, Paul Bambrick-Santoyo suggests prioritizing feedback meetings that directly follow classroom observations.[3] When studying his work under the leadership of Debbie McFalone, an incredible Michigan educator, friend, and mentor, I revamped our school's observation protocols and began scheduling feedback meetings first. This way, teachers knew I would be observing them twenty-four to forty-eight hours before our feedback meetings, and they could trust that they would get prompt feedback because the meeting was already scheduled. As a principal, seeing teachers and students in action is important, but it means nothing to that individual teacher without feedback—and one-way feedback is not nearly as effective as two-way feedback in person. Written feedback, such as emails or checklists, gives the evaluator an opportunity to communicate with the teacher, but it doesn't give the teacher an opportunity to respond in a meaningful way. If you'd like to learn more about how these concepts were incorporated into the observation system at Quincy Elementary, please visit AllysonApsey.com.

Tell the teacher the good stuff and ask about the bad stuff.

One of the best pieces of advice new principals can get is from George Couros, an educational leader, speaker, and author, as well as a friend. The first time I heard George speak was at a MEMSPA (Michigan Elementary and Middle School Principals Association) state conference in Kalamazoo (it's a real place, trust me), in December of 2015. There, George said that new leaders must discover a strength of every teacher before making any changes during the first months of their principalship. Veteran principals, can you name a strength of each one of your teachers? Do your teachers know that you see this strength in them? And are you looking for new emerging strengths every time you

---

3 Paul Bambrick-Santoyo, *Leverage Leadership: A Practical Guide to Building Exceptional Schools* (San Francisco: Jossey-Bass, 2012), 61–62.

observe them? The feedback meeting provides a wonderful opportunity to highlight all the big and little strengths you observe. Be as specific as possible, and focus on the impact these strengths have on students.

We know that teachers are incredibly hard on themselves, and most teachers are very reflective. When principals observe teachers in action, we want to identify next steps for the teacher so we can help propel them to the next level. Whether we observe something we are concerned about or have an idea for growth, it's best to first ask the teacher a question about the topic to give them an opportunity to share their thinking. Often, they have already identified the concern, and this question can serve as a launchpad to help them make an action plan. When posed as a question, feedback that could have been perceived as criticism and crushed the teacher is instead a team effort to help the teacher grow.

Don't create a "dog and pony show."

There are so many reasons to avoid making teacher observation feel like a dog and pony show. First, it does not give evaluators an accurate picture of the daily learning in the classroom. Second, it places unnecessary stress on a teacher. We want teachers' focus to remain on students and their learning, not on principals coming in to observe. A simple way to accomplish this is to have most observations be drop-ins. When I schedule the feedback meetings, the only thing the teacher knows is that I will be observing them sometime within twenty-four to forty-eight hours before our meeting. When structuring observations this way, it takes deliberate effort from principals to make sure they observe at different times and for different subjects or classes throughout the year to get a complete picture.

In addition to drop-ins, I like to offer teachers an opportunity to ask me to come in and observe a particular lesson. When a teacher asks me to come in for a lesson they're excited about, I know it's because of the student learning and engagement. This requested observation can be used as part of the teacher evaluation process or for informal feedback, depending on what the teacher is looking for in the feedback. For example, sometimes teachers invite me in because they're trying something new and want my input. I don't want fear of the evaluation score to interfere with innovating and risk taking, so I'm happy to visit to just give informal feedback.

Do not make the evaluation process extra work.

I cringe when a teacher from another district tells me they were up late completing their pre-observation forms. First, our teachers need rest. Second, if they spend their precious evenings working, it better be on something that makes a major difference for students. Maybe some pre-observation protocols for teachers check that box, but none I have ever seen do.

Teachers work hard both inside and outside the classroom. We need to look at what we can remove from their plates rather than add to them. Planning and reflecting are crucial to professional development, but focusing those efforts on collective teacher efficacy rather than mindlessly filling out forms and checking boxes would be a much better use of teacher time.

End by summing up the main points.

If you read ten emails singing your praises and one that has a stinging criticism, which do you remember? Teachers are the same way.

Some leaders like to use the sandwich method when giving feedback. For those of you unfamiliar with this method, it is when we sandwich a criticism between two compliments. This causes a lot of problems. Can we toast the sandwich method? (See what I did there?) First, the recipient of this baloney sandwich only remembers the criticism. Second, regular users of this method will find their listeners always waiting for the other shoe to drop, which means they won't even hear the compliment—even when it isn't followed by criticism. Third, the sandwich method makes the evaluator feel better but doesn't make the teacher feel any better.

Instead, have an honest conversation where you highlight strengths, ask questions to promote growth, and help the teacher plan their next steps. Then, before you end the meeting, ask the teacher to sum up the main points of the conversation. Carolyn McKanders, a cognitive coaching trainer, author, and director emeritus of Thinking Collaborative, shared in a training session that learning is not complete until debriefing or reflecting has taken place. Giving the teacher an opportunity to sum up the main points of the conversation solidifies the teacher's learning, and it's great modeling for best practice in the classroom.

It can go something like this:

Principal: Wow! That was a great conversation. I am so proud of where you are and where you're going. We said a lot, so let's wrap up with a summary. What are the main points you're taking away from our conversation?

Teacher: [shares areas for growth and action plan but omits strengths discussed]

Principal: Yes! I'm excited about your plan and ready to help you. However, you left out some important points we talked about. What are the strengths we discussed?

Teacher: [blushing] Oh yeah, I forgot to mention those. Well . . .

One of the most important parts of the feedback conversation is the summary at the end, especially when there are significant areas for growth. After a summary like this, the teacher will feel empowered and leave with clear direction. Please note that it is important for the teacher to do the summing up because the person who is talking is the person who is thinking.

Dolly Parton wrote, "If your actions create a legacy that inspires others to dream more, learn more, do more and become more, then you are an excellent leader." If principals can use evaluations to build relationships with teachers while helping them see strengths and plan for continuous improvement, this gives us an opportunity to make teacher evaluation an empowerment tool rather than something to be feared.

TEACHER APPRECIATION ALL YEAR LONG

I love providing meals, treats, and surprises for staff all year long. We make a big deal out of Teacher Appreciation Week and the weeks leading up to the winter holidays. Educational leaders from around the country share fabulous ideas to help teachers feel appreciated, and so many of the ideas I've implemented have been harvested from others. Derek Wheaton, one of my favorite educational leaders in Michigan, taught me the concept of harvesting ideas rather than stealing them. I love this and just try to be sure to give appropriate credit.

Amber Teamann and Melinda Miller, two incredible educational leaders, wrote a book called *Lead with Appreciation: Fostering a Culture of Gratitude*, and they have inspired leaders across the world with the appreciation ideas they share. If you need ways to make your staff feel special and appreciated, I encourage you to check out their book. The Principals in Action group of educational leaders across the country is another source of great ideas. You can join the Principals in Action Facebook group or find them on Twitter using the #PrincipalsinAction hashtag.

CELEBRATE WINS, BIG OR SMALL

Did your students rock their recent state assessment? Wonderful! Celebrate by sharing a birthday-style sheet cake and sparkling juice. Just be careful. If you focus all your big celebrations on assessment data, you may be sending an unintended message that one-shot, high-stakes testing is the most important thing in your school.

Let's think through some other reasons to celebrate:

- Teachers supported each other through a quick shift to virtual learning.
- Student behavior referrals decreased after a new SEL curriculum was implemented.
- A parent sent a note of appreciation about how welcome they feel in your school.
- You made it through assessment season, report cards, and conferences!

TEACHER APPRECIATION JUST BECAUSE

Prove to staff that you appreciate them every day, not just on special occasions. Here is a list of ways to incorporate teacher appreciation and celebrations throughout the school year:

- Implement Workout Wear Mondays to help make Monday the best day of the week. This not only encourages staff to dress comfortably and get on the floor with students, but it also promotes incorporating movement into the school day. Special shout-out to educational leader Sean Gaillard for his leadership with the #CelebrateMonday movement.
- Walk a snack cart full of staff favorites around the school and interrupt staff members to step into the hall and grab a sweet or salty snack. They are often interrupted for not-so-great things, so it's fun to surprise them with a wonderful and yummy interruption.
- Create a staff Zen Zone. On especially busy days (like Halloween, field day, Valentine's Day), I would vacate my office and transform it into a Zen Zone for staff. They can find soft music, aromatherapy, dim lighting, spa treatments, and healthy snacks and beverages. This gives them an opportunity to meet several of their five basic needs (love and belonging, freedom, power, fun, and survival).

- Write little notes of appreciation. I see handwritten notes posted behind teachers' desks years after I wrote them. There is something special about handwritten notes with specific positive feedback, but even if you only have time for a quick email or voice mail, just do it. If you think something positive about someone, take action and share that positive feedback. You will never regret that decision.
- Have chocolate available at all times. Now, I said I wouldn't mention food much in this book about supporting teachers, but having chocolate available for staff at all times should just be a given. Enough said.
- Cook for your teachers. I am not good at this one because I'm a terrible cook, but I love the idea of a leader whipping up a pancake breakfast or cooking hamburgers on the grill for lunch. I don't put this idea into practice much, but I aspire to.
- Share books with your teachers. My friend and educational leader Jessica Gomez buys her staff inspiring picture books frequently. This is a quadruple win because it shows her teachers how much she thinks of and appreciates them, it models a love for literacy, the chosen books often incorporate SEL or diversity, and the students benefit when the teacher shares the books with them.

APPRECIATE BY WALKING AROUND

Whenever I'm out and about in the school, I'm always in the right place at the right time. The concept of managing by walking around is nothing new—it dates back to executives at Hewlett-Packard in the 1970s. We know that walking around and connecting with people one-on-one helps leaders build relationships and understand the challenges and successes staff are having. What if we focus on showing appreciation as we walk around by sharing feedback in the form of affective statements? It is incredibly powerful to get specific feedback that highlights the impact of the teacher's behavior. A key concept in restorative practices is using affective statements where we share how we have been affected by someone's behavior. The benefit is that it reinforces the specific positive outcome of the behavior, which is powerful and specific feedback that results in the likelihood that the behavior will be repeated. Here are some examples of affective feedback:

- I am grateful that you prioritize small-group instruction. It is not easy to always fit it in, but your students are really benefiting from the specialized instruction and interaction with you.
- I am inspired by your read-alouds with students. You choose books with powerful SEL messages, and the way you read is so engaging! I need to watch you more often to help me prep for my Facebook Live read-alouds.
- It brings me such joy to watch you interact with your colleagues. You generously share ideas and lessons, you empower them by asking for their feedback and implementing their ideas, and you are so kind and patient.

I know that educators reading this book share my passion for making sure all teachers and school staff feel valued. This is a crucial step in leading the whole teacher and making school a safe, need-satisfying place for them.

IDEAS TO IMPLEMENT TOMORROW:

- As you read the section on teacher evaluation and observation, what stories came to mind from your experience as a teacher or leader? When you reflect on your own stories, what call to action comes to mind? Spend a few moments journaling your thoughts and ideas.
- What ideas do you have to empower teachers through evaluation, and what is your next step in using evaluation as a

teacher empowerment tool? Visit AllysonApsey.com to download a checklist to help you get started.

- Choose one way to show teachers that there's no place you'd rather be than in their classrooms watching them do what they do best.
- Pick one idea from the section on showing teacher appreciation all year long to implement right away. Will you show appreciation by walking around? Will you celebrate a win while being cognizant of any unintended messages it might send? Or will you plan a surprise for staff just because?
- Share your own ideas with the #LeadingtheWholeTeacher community on social media.

QUESTIONS FOR COLLABORATION AND REFLECTION:

- What did you relate to in my story about using the word *lackadaisical* in a teacher evaluation?

- What is an area of strength in your evaluation process? What is your next step in making evaluation and observation a teacher empowerment tool?

- When reading the section on teacher appreciation, what connections did you make? What changes are you considering?

CHAPTER 5

BUILDING POSITIVE RELATIONSHIPS

There is no exercise better for the heart than reaching down and lifting people up.

—John Andrew Holmes

began working when I was fifteen years old, and I've never stopped. I had some interesting jobs before I started my educational career. But whether I was serving up fried chicken, gluing fabric swatches into sample books, or selling shoes, every workplace had a consistent theme: no matter the working conditions or the disgusting jobs I might be asked to do, I was happiest in the places where there were good relationships among the staff. It was helpful to learn early on that it wasn't always *what* I did that equated to enjoying my jobs—it was *who* I worked with. Inevitably, every single time the focus on relationships started at the top.

My personal findings are not surprising because they are supported by research: positive work relationships lead to job satisfaction. A 2014 Gallup poll found that employees who reported high well-being including positive relationships were 59 percent less likely to look for a new job within the next twelve months.[1] The school leader cannot do this work alone; it takes a group effort among all the staff. Teacher leaders are key in this effort to create a school where the staff functions as an uplifting and supportive team.

FOSTERING POSITIVE STAFF RELATIONSHIPS

Recently I reread Brené Brown's *Dare to Lead* in anticipation of participating in the Daring Teams workshops with our district administration team. In the book, Brené shares four skill sets of daring leadership: rumbling with vulnerability, living your values (rather than simply professing them), braving trust (and being the first to trust), and learning to rise.[2] The skill set that spoke loudest to me this time around was living your values.

In the book, Brené tells a story about her CFO.[3] When he'd question her about big risks she wanted to take, she thought it meant he didn't trust her. However, she came to understand that his questions were about his core value of financial stability and not about her at all. This really helped their relationship. This story got me thinking about the staff at our school. What if they knew each other's two core values so they could better understand the motivation behind their behavior? What might that mean for staff relationships?

Brené suggests that whittling down our list of important values to our two core values helps us reflect on the motivation for our own behavior, helps others understand us better, and helps us understand how we might make effective changes in our lives. This exercise was powerful for me, and I wanted to share what I was learning with our staff. I developed a set of exercises based on Brené's work, listed below.

---

1 Dan Witters and Sangeeta Agrawal, "Well-Being Enhances Benefits of Employee Engagement," October 27, 2015, Gallup, gallup.com/workplace/236483/enhances-benefits-employee-engagement.aspx.

2 Brown, *Dare to Lead*, 11.

3 Brown, *Dare to Lead*, 208.

BUILDING RELATIONSHIPS
THROUGH SHARING VALUES

Step 1: Be aware of your own core values.

We know that we need self-awareness to move forward with a new idea, though we don't always practice it. As the leader of a school, I must first recognize my own core values, so I downloaded Brené's list of over a hundred values (found on the Dare to Lead hub on BreneBrown.com) to whittle the list down to my two core values. Values such as integrity, joy, service, and health are included in the list. It's a hard exercise and helped me to recognize that naming my two core values does not mean I don't have other values, too. My core values are integrity and making a difference, and since I named them my eyes have opened. I see areas where I lean into my values and where I can work on leaning into them more.

Step 2: Guide your staff in naming their core values.

During a staff meeting, teachers can go through the exercise of defining their values. This can be accomplished in a group setting, or the exercise can be introduced to the group and then teachers can work through it on their own. (Visit AllysonApsey.com to find a slideshow to introduce the idea.) Once teachers have identified their two core values and a trusting environment has been established (through previous work with relationship building), they can share them with each other. In her book, Brené talks about an activity where staff members wrote their names and values on chart paper and hung them around the room. Others then wrote positive comments about the person and how they lived their values. You can get creative with this. The whole process could take place during one staff meeting, or the papers could stay up on the walls in the staff lounge for a week to give teachers time to write comments. You can also do this activity virtually with Google

Slides and have each staff member create a slide for themselves with their name and their core values.

Step 3: Reflect on what it means to understand each other's core values.

After working through the values self-awareness process, it's helpful to circle back to the concept for some reflection. At the next staff meeting, ask this simple question: "What does knowing each other's core values mean for us?" This gives teachers an opportunity to share how this practice has changed them and the school culture for the better. In a virtual meeting you could use a tool like Mentimeter or Google Jamboard to allow teachers to share. If you're sharing at an in-person meeting, you could give teachers an opportunity to talk about the question in small groups and then share. Or they could spend a few minutes writing a reflection before sharing their thoughts with the whole group. This time for reflection is a crucial part of the next step.

Step 4: Determine your school's core values.

Wouldn't it be a wonderful world if staff could work together to define the school's core values? You can take the self-awareness process and mirror it in small groups to whittle the list of values down to core values for the school. Years ago we worked through a similar process process to define who we are as the Q-Crew, the staff of Quincy Elementary. We came up with an acrostic where each letter of Quincy represents one of our values.

At Quincy, our Q-Nique framework could help us go through Brené's list of values to choose the core values that shape everything we do at our school. We may not be able to narrow it down to just two, but we would be OK with settling on three or four. However, it's important to keep in mind that the clearer the target, the more likely we are to hit it. And it's helpful for all stakeholders to have a voice in this process—*all* staff, students, and even families. What tools might you use at

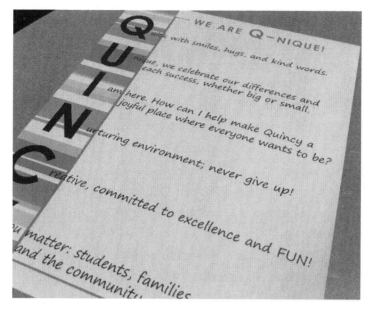

your school as you select your collective core values? You can consider referencing a mission, vision statement, or your collective agreements on how you will interact with each other.

Once the values of the school are identified, the first step in living them is to define what they look like in each setting at the school. If one of the core values of the school is belonging, describe what that looks like in every area of the school. What does belonging look like in the staff lounge? In staff meetings? In the school office? What does it look like when interacting with students? In a math lesson? Revisiting these descriptions frequently will help staff live the school values and will support strong, positive relationships.

It is important that the values and associated behaviors are recorded, displayed, and frequently revisited. It is beneficial to redefine how the core values look and sound in the various areas and roles in the school each year. They could be displayed in a conference room where you frequently have meetings, in the staff lounge, in the mail room, or all the above. It can also be beneficial to talk about nonexamples of the values. For instance, if your school values connection, that does not look like gossip in the staff lounge.

FOSTERING RELATIONSHIPS THROUGH TEAM BUILDING

I have the honor of coaching new school leaders, and one of the conversations I had before a recent school year began was about team-building activities at staff meetings. The new leader was worried that some staff members would roll their eyes about "fluffy" team-building activities. On the one hand, the concerns are understandable—time is a precious commodity, and teachers may not see the value in doing team building for team building's sake. On the other hand, we know that staff need opportunities to get to know one another, they need to laugh together to have great relationships, and our time together is limited, so we need to enhance our bonds whenever we can. The new leader and I devised a solution that just might work for everyone: team building with multiple purposes. Here's a list of some of the ideas we generated:

- Play a game that helps staff members learn each other's names.
- Turn reviewing procedural information into a fun activity.
- Teach several games that staff members can use with students. (They won't even know they are team building as they practice them!)
- Have small groups get creative solving a problem in a unique way, and then share their solutions with everyone.
- Insert the team-building activity into the middle of the meeting to disguise it even further.
- Make collaboration the norm in staff meetings so it becomes "just the way we do things."

FOSTERING RELATIONSHIPS THROUGH SOCIAL EVENTS

In my previous school, we hosted Be There or Be Square activities for staff once per month. They were planned by different groups throughout the school, and we welcomed anyone who could attend and understood when staff members couldn't make it. We tried to plan different types of activities to appeal to as many staff members as possible. A core group of staff members showed up to nearly every event, some only came when they could or when the activity interested them, and a few never came at all for various reasons. Even with spotty attendance, it was still worth it. Some staff need those social connections more than others, and that is OK.

At Quincy Elementary, where I was the luckiest principal in the world, we did some outside-of-school social activities, but we prioritized social opportunities at school so we could involve as many staff members as possible. One of our traditions was Wonderful Wednesday, when we all had about fifteen minutes to socialize over a shared snack provided by a different staff member or group of staff members each week. This was an optional activity for both the snack providers and snack partakers, but it was a cherished tradition for all of us. We did this with some creative planning for recess supervision or right after or right before school started. We loved that this relationship-building social time was accessible to almost everyone each week.

FOSTERING RELATIONSHIPS THROUGH RESOLVING (AND PREVENTING) CONFLICTS

Years and years ago, my sister and I signed up to walk a marathon and raise money for the Leukemia Society of America. Months of training and fundraising culminated in a trip to Hawaii to walk the Honolulu Marathon. Our young and fit selves walked about as fast as I can run a mile these days, so it wasn't a leisurely stroll. It was hard work.

I love my sister now and I loved her then, but at one point in the race we were focused more on bickering with each other than on the race itself. We were hot and chafing and tired and really irritable, and we were hitting elbows once in a while, which led to the bickering.

Someone from the Leukemia Society of America team even noticed and encouraged us to uplift each other. Even in the most loving and supportive relationships, when we are working really hard side by side, we can get irritated with each other from time to time.

Remember the word cloud created by teachers that listed gossip as the number one reason teachers don't feel safe at school? While this chapter's suggestions will help foster strong, positive relationships at school, which will prevent many relational problems, we all know that conflicts will still arise. When they do, it is incredibly important to address issues rather than push them under the rug. When little irritations or conflicts go unaddressed, they tend to add up and result in a big explosion or argument that could have been prevented. Or they result in a team member withdrawing from the team. Or worse, that team member leaves the school or profession altogether.

Here's a simple guide to addressing issues in a relatively comfortable way that incorporates strategies I have learned and honed over the years. Trust me, I benefit from revisiting these tips from time to time. This process can be used when addressing culture-harming behaviors like gossip, persistent negativity, and unhealthy competition.

- **Express how you feel.** Start the conversation by expressing how you feel. Often, we think others can guess how we feel, but in reality they don't know unless we tell them. Unknowingly, people can be very unaware of how their behavior is impacting others. Speak only for yourself and never go into a conversation claiming that you represent a group.
  - "I was a little hurt when you . . ."
  - "I wasn't sure what you meant by . . ."
  - "I felt surprised when . . ."

- **Avoid inflammatory words.** Avoid words that make the problem seem bigger than it is. Don't use words like *always*, *worst*, *terrible*, etc. Instead focus on addressing the specific problem to keep it as small as possible.

- **Spritz on some "naïve body spray."** Go into the conversation with the naïve assumption that your teammate has no idea that they offended you and would never intend to be offensive. This is likely true, and this generous assumption will help your teammate not get defensive, which will help as you work on resolving the issue. Make sure you explicitly say that you know they would never intend to hurt you.
- **Pause.** Give your teammate time to respond and share their feelings before you dive into problem solving. Again, we cannot assume we know how our colleague is feeling. If necessary, ask a question to prompt them. You can ask, "What are you thinking and feeling?" It's important that all the information about your unique perspectives is on the table before you head into problem solving.
- **Problem solve.** Gather ideas for solutions from both sides and then determine the solution you can both live with. This process can start with a simple question like "Where do we go from here?" For the solution to stick, both of you need to leave the conversation feeling heard, understood, and confident in the outcome.

In addition, it may be helpful to brainstorm as a staff how to address issues such as gossip. One idea is to have a common response to gossip, an agreed-upon mantra. You could say, "At our school we talk *to* people, not *about* people." Or as a reminder you could ask, "Did you talk to [insert name] about this?"

Naïve Body Spray

Do you wish that you could easily take the naïve approach and assume that all people want good things for themselves rather than making inaccurate or negative assumptions?

Your dreams can come true

for the low, low cost of $9.99 plus S/H.

One daily spritz of the incredible Naïve Body Spray will have you assuming positive intentions from the people around you all day long! As a bonus, if you order now, we will include a second Naïve Body Spray disguised as bathroom air freshener to help out your grumpy coworkers!

Don't delay, act today by calling 1-800-SpritzMe!

FOSTERING POSITIVE CONNECTIONS THROUGHOUT THE SCHOOL COMMUNITY

Strong, positive relationships among the staff and between leaders and staff set the stage for strong, positive relationships with students and families as well. Although our focus in this chapter is strong relationships among staff, remember that all relationships throughout the school community are important. Incorporating social-emotional learning into the curriculum to teach students how to regulate their own behavior and how to develop great relationships with others is crucial.

Clear and frequent communication with families invites them into the school day even when they cannot be there in person. It is the school staff's responsibility to tell the story of the school or district. A lack of information makes our minds go to negative places, so we need to highlight all the amazing things happening in our schools—that's the story people need to know.

IDEAS TO IMPLEMENT TOMORROW:

- Ask a few teachers what helps them build strong, positive relationships with each other and create next steps based on their feedback.
- Define your own core values and reflect on how they influence your leadership. What might happen if your staff knew your core values? Brainstorm ways you might share your core values with staff.
- Start your next staff meeting with a doubleheader—an activity that builds relationships *and* moves your staff toward a goal.
- Plan a Be There or Be Square event alongside a group of staff members. Don't be afraid to think outside the box: after-school yard games, snacks, or meeting up to race go-karts at a local amusement park. You could keep it simple by inviting all staff to eat lunch outside and providing blankets and popsicles, or

you could go all-out and attend a local professional sporting event together.

- Revisit the word cloud your staff created when you asked what makes them feel unsafe at your school. (Or insert this into your next staff meeting if you haven't asked yet.) What might be your next (or first) action step to help equip teachers with conflict resolution skills?

- Share your ideas for fostering strong relationships with the #LeadingtheWholeTeacher community on social media.

QUESTIONS FOR COLLABORATION AND REFLECTION:

- What is your school's mission and vision? How is it fulfilled in every part of the building? What are your next steps in this area?

- Thinking back over the jobs you've had, what is one common theme among the jobs you loved? What impact might that have on your current workplace?

- What are the next steps you can take to support your school's teachers in conflict resolution?

CHAPTER 6

PROTECTING HEALTHY WORKLOADS

Time and health are two precious assets that we don't recognize and appreciate until they have been depleted.

—Denis Waitley

The idea of helping teachers find more balance and shoulder healthy workloads is necessary and perplexing at the same time. It is necessary because the frantic pace of education is not sustainable, as evidenced by the hours teachers put in to meet the increasing demands of our profession. Whether it's hours of parent-teacher conferences after teaching all day, putting your classroom back together after a dysregulated student destroyed it for the umpteenth time, or yet again talking a colleague off the ledge because she is so distraught, the workload and the worry load are taking a toll: an increasing number of educators are leaving the profession, and there's a lack of college students pursuing education degrees. Yet, it is perplexing to define what a healthy workload looks like for educators because it looks a bit different for each person.

DEFINING WHAT A HEALTHY WORKLOAD LOOKS LIKE FOR EDUCATORS

Feeling overworked and stressed out seems to be accepted as the norm for educators. Let's explore this question: Does it have to be this way?

If not, what steps can we take to improve the quality of life for teachers so they can do the job they love and be healthy—both mentally and physically? How can we help them feel fulfilled in their work and in their personal lives? How can we reduce educator workloads and stress?

The journey to protecting our teachers' time and capacity by making their workloads more manageable starts with defining some universal truths of healthy workloads. Here's what happens when our workloads are manageable and healthy:

- **We feel in control.** Teaching is hard work; it always has been and always will be. Being an educator is not for the faint of heart. We give big, we feel big, and we have servant hearts. But we did not sign up for constantly feeling overwhelmed. Having a healthy workload means we feel in control of our time both in school and out of school. Instead of feeling frenzied and controlled by deadlines, we have the freedom to prioritize what needs to be done first.

- **We have space for creativity and connecting.** Educators are creative and full of new ideas to support students and learning. Wouldn't it be wonderful to have the time to make our creative ideas come alive? To have a need-satisfying environment, we require time to make connections with colleagues and students. Having a healthy workload means we have space in our workday to make both of those things happen.

- **We choose whether we work at night or on weekends.** Some educators love spending a few hours at night or on the weekends catching up on email, grading, reading for professional purposes, exploring Pinterest for their classroom, etc.

This is perfectly fine, and they should not feel guilty about it. Educators should, however, feel like working on the weekends and in the evenings is optional. The problem is when they feel like the only way they can keep their heads above water is by spending eight hours at school on the weekends and bringing a couple of hours' worth of work home every weeknight.

SUPPORTING TEACHER WELLNESS

When my good friend and incredible educational leader Brad Gustafson (@GustafsonBrad) heard I was writing this book, he recommended that I connect with Beth Joselyn, an elementary art teacher at his school, Greenwood Elementary School, in Plymouth, Minnesota. Beth is a leader within their school in supporting staff self-care. I am thrilled that she was willing to share her perspective and helpful tools with us.

TEACHER PERSPECTIVE ON SELF-CARE BY BETH JOSELYN

When COVID-19 hit, teachers began hearing the term *self-care* over and over. For many of us, that term has vague connotations of guilt and shame. We didn't know where to begin or what self-care meant to us.

"I don't have time for self-care!" my colleagues said. Worse yet, it became a sarcastic comment between teachers as they frantically and exhaustedly tried to manage their never-ending workload. We reacted this way because suddenly we were told to prioritize self-care without being told what that means. This lack of clarity created even more of a disconnect and room for resentment.

To avoid this, leaders can support and build a community of staff that prioritizes self-care in three ways:

1. Lead by example. It is crucial for a leader to practice their own self-care. This creates trust with staff because they see and feel the effects of a leader who truly walks the walk with a routine self-care practice.

2. Offer PD and training on self-care. Spas, massages, and even downtime can support self-care, but the foundation of it is more personal and incremental. It helps to create a space for these whole-staff conversations to occur. As leaders, if we arbitrarily choose the self-care *for* our staff, we miss the opportunity to create a meaningful self-care culture driven by actual staff needs. Leaders can optimize the self-care PD by choosing specific topics relevant to the school community.

3. Bring the self-care conversation and learning into the classroom. Once self-care has been defined within the learning community, we need to spread the word to our students, too! We don't need to wait until our students are gone for the day to practice our self-care; instead, we can create an environment where we can practice *with* our students. Incorporating activities such as mindful breathing, movement, opportunities for laughter, social connections, and self-compassion strategies will help students feel good and be ready for learning. And practicing right along with students can help teachers feel good, too. Internal harmony can spread throughout the classroom. As Resmaa Menakem said, "A settled body has the capacity to harmonize the unsettled body."

Our society has been running on fumes because of the "work more, longer, harder, faster" mentality. The pressure educators feel to perform conflicts with the notion of self-care. As such, we need to retrain our brains to understand that self-care doesn't need to take a lot of time, and it doesn't need to be a *this* or *that* but an *and* equation—we can meet our obligations *and* take care of ourselves.

"If it's gonna be, it's up to me!"

Self-care begins with our nervous system. Left unattended, our nervous system takes on a life all its own, and we are along for the ride. We are on a roller coaster of stress chemicals, and we don't even know it. This can quickly lead to feeling overwhelmed and reaching a state of burnout (i.e., end-of-the-day exhaustion). This does not need to happen. We can intentionally practice resetting our nervous system throughout the day, and by doing so, we can leave work refreshed and ready for what's next.

As a younger teacher I often left school with headaches and no energy, feeling continually overwhelmed. At one point I wondered how long I could continue to teach. Then I began training at the Center for Mind-Body Medicine under the guidance of James S. Gordon, MD, and his staff, who specialize in healing trauma states through mind-body practices. As I learned more about the nervous system and practices that aid in healing trauma states, I began to see an overlap in the symptoms of trauma states and teacher burnout. I started using some of the practices I learned from my training in my daily life and quickly saw and felt the results.

My headaches stopped, and after I left school I had new energy to utilize in other areas of my life. I also had more patience and joy throughout the day. I found that if I sprinkled in practices in short increments, my whole system (brain and body) felt more connected, activated, and rejuvenated.

I wanted to share this information with every teacher I knew, so I created a system of short practices. The result is two-minute self-care strategies based on over twelve years of mind-body training, self-study, and field testing.

To help the practitioner customize these strategies for their needs, I have broken them down into the following three categories:

- **Heart intelligence practice helps us zoom out and see the bigger world around us.** It helps with connection and relationships with yourself and others.
- **Stillness practice supports us by clearing the clutter from our brain and helps us with feeling overwhelmed.** I tell my students, "Stillness is a superpower, and it takes skill to be still." Practice makes stillness possible.
- **Intentional movement activates our energy and awakens our state of being.** These practices are great to do after lunch and before classroom transitions.

Here is an example of each practice.

Heart intelligence practice: heart check (30–90 seconds)
Find a moment during the day to take the following steps:

1. Pause.
2. Find stillness.
3. Focus on the space around your heart.
4. Feel your breath.
5. Notice as you relax into your breathing pattern that your heart feels like it is expanding.
6. Notice your shoulders begin to relax.
7. Think about a gift you received:
   - A smile
   - A willing listener
   - A laugh
8. Feel the impact of that as you open your eyes to the moment. You may notice you feel different:
   - Calmer
   - Lighter
   - Brighter

Stillness practice: 4-7-8 anchor breathing (90–120 seconds)

Throughout the day, try to find time to take the following steps:

1. Find a place to sit where you can position your spine to be loosely straight.
2. Position your feet on the floor, facing forward and parallel (our brain likes symmetry).
3. Tilt your pelvis forward slightly.
4. Inhale with your chest up.
5. Move your shoulders up, back, and down so your shoulder blades hug your spine.
6. Keep your chin parallel to the floor.
7. Place your hands on your thighs and rest your elbows by your waist.
8. Relax your jaw.
9. Notice how your spine and lungs are in the perfect position to receive the benefits of stillness.
10. Use your breath as an anchor, and repeat the following breath pattern four to eight times:
    - 4-count inhale
    - 7-count hold
    - 8-count exhale
11. After the final round, feel your stillness and notice the calming effects in your body.
12. Thank yourself for this present moment. (This part is important—honoring ourselves for showing up for ourselves.)

Intentional movement: six spine movements (45–60 seconds)

This can be done on the hour and has lasting effects such as more energy, less achy joints, increased creativity, easier access to problem-solving skills—the list goes on and on. Here's how to incorporate intentional movement into your day:

1. To begin, follow these instructions:
   - Stand tall.
   - Place your feet together with your toes and heels touching.
   - Hold your arms up over your head.
   - Press your palms together.
   - Interlock your fingers.
   - Release your index fingers.
   - Cross your thumbs and grip tight.
2. Stretch up and bend your body to the right (opening up the left side of your body).
3. Bend your body to the left (opening up the right side of your body).
4. Return to center.
5. Look up at your hands. This creates a tiny backbend in your upper back.
6. Fold forward. You can bend your knees as much as you want.
7. Hang there for a bit.
8. Relax your head down, then shake it yes and shake it no.
9. Shrug your shoulders.
10. Tuck your chin against your chest and come up slowly.
11. Focus on one vertebra at a time.
12. Lift your chin up last.
13. Keep your feet together and pointing forward as you twist your upper body to the right.
14. Feel the twist.
15. Twist your upper body to the left.
16. Feel the twist.
17. And just like that, find that you are kinder, smarter, and clearer on your next action!

Like Beth shared, it is important to emphasize staff wellness and self-care that goes beyond jeans days, chocolate, and pizza. Wellness is key in reducing the worry load that staff members carry. As I mentioned in chapter 4, one of the ways we have supported staff wellness at our school is by creating a Zen Zone for staff. Before I confiscated an office to create a permanent Zen Zone, I gave up my own office frequently. Now Quincy Elementary has a permanent Zen Zone where staff can escape, rejuvenate, self-regulate, recharge, or even take a quick nap (find the Leading the Whole Teacher tab in the "Books" section on AllysonApsey.com to watch a video). This space also works great for nursing moms who need to pump because it has a door that locks and can be used as a private space.

Not all staff members take advantage of this space, but just knowing it's there for them can help the school be a need-satisfying place. We ask teachers to provide a place in the classroom where students can go if they need to escape and regulate their emotions, and it's great modeling to have a similar space for teachers. The staff lounge often serves many purposes because it is work space, eating space, and socializing space, and it's too busy and loud for to be considered a Zen Zone retreat.

EMAIL IS A BLESSING AND A CURSE

We communicate through email and texts more than any other mode of communication. This can be efficient, and it's helpful to be able to read and send messages when we have the time. Unfortunately, it can result in us feeling the need to be constantly connected. And sometimes it feels like we must go through an email with a fine-tooth comb to find the point. As leaders, it is important to wield the power of email carefully and use it for good rather than evil.

EMAIL TO INSPIRE, NOT BAFFLE

Have you ever checked your email and groaned for one of these reasons?

- You see your boss is in communication mode, so you know you will have a barrage of emails from them. While leading a school, teaching students, preparing for the next day, communicating with parents, etc., you are supposed to read each email thoroughly and remember everything you read.
- You open an email with trepidation, one eye open and one eye closed, because you know every email from this person is the length of a novel.
- You carefully read an email searching and searching for the main message, but you cannot filter all the words to glean it.

Leaders can avoid being the reason for the "email groan" by taking the advice of some famous writers.

Brevity is the soul of wit.
—William Shakespeare

Implement the no-scroll rule for all your emails. Your message should fit on the screen and not require the recipient to scroll. Getting right to the point, skipping unnecessary words or information, or limiting the number of topics in an email can help you implement this rule.

Clarity is the counterbalance of profound thoughts.
—Luc de Clapiers

Use the subject line to communicate the main message of the email. This helps your staff avoid the guessing game by making the point of the email crystal clear.

The two most powerful warriors are
patience and time.

—Leo Tolstoy

Save it up and send a weekly memo. Some principals send a Monday memo or a Friday update to share important information with staff members. If you're tempted to press Send on an email, ask yourself if it can wait for the Friday update. Nine times out of ten, it can. Besides the benefit to staff inboxes, this also makes your weekly communication meatier and therefore increases readership.

Variety's the very spice of life,
that gives it all its flavor.

—William Cowper

Use a variety of communication techniques: make funny videos, start a podcast for staff, write handwritten notes, etc. Novelty and variety benefit staff just like they benefit students.

These thoughtful email practices will help you become a model of effective communication and garner gratitude and respect from your staff. Words are a leader's most important tool, so wield them carefully.

SEVEN REASONS TO NOT SEND EMAIL ON WEEKENDS

I am as guilty as anyone of working on the weekends. It's weird, though: I used to be able to spend a couple of hours working on a Saturday morning and then disconnect for the rest of the weekend. Ever since COVID-19 shut us down, however, I feel the need to stay connected to work 24-7. I know I am not alone: You feel the same way, don't you? The umbilical cord that seems to keep us connected all the time is email. Even though I try to disconnect on the weekend, I find myself checking email constantly. I have to literally put my phone away, on airplane mode, to stop myself. And that only works sometimes.

As a school principal, I know staff feel the need to stay connected the same way I do. But it's not healthy. We are more than educators. We are parents, aunts, brothers, friends, cousins, and whole people. The facets of our lives other than school deserve our attention, preferably every evening and all weekend. And if we can't get away from email entirely on weeknights, it would be wonderful to know that we don't have to worry about group emails on the weekends. Here are seven reasons to avoid sending emails on weekends:

1. **We model self-care.** Like Beth Joselyn shared, one of the most important things a leader can do is model self-care. At times in my career, it has felt like a competition for who could work the most hours, and that is not a healthy way to live. Prioritizing self-care and friends and family on the weekend helps us refresh and renew for the week ahead, and that helps us do our best work for our students. We must take care of ourselves before we can take care of others.

2. **We increase the chances that our emails will be read.** When I get a lengthy group email on a Saturday night, I open it, ask myself why the person sent it then, and then work hard to forget about it while I focus on my family. Then, I get busy on Monday morning, new emails come in, and before I know it, that Saturday night email is truly buried and forgotten. If you want your email messages to be read and acted upon, it is helpful to send them when teachers will likely be reading email. For example, send it midmorning on Monday so they will see it when they check their email at lunch. Or send it midafternoon so they will read it before leaving for the night.

3. **We communicate respect.** How many times have we read a weekend work email that starts with this: "I hope you aren't reading this until Monday morning . . ." We chuckle because *of*

course we're checking our email at 10:30 p.m. on Friday night! Holding off on email during the weekend sends a message that we respect people's downtime. It's like saying, "I care enough about you to not risk interrupting your precious weekend, so I will schedule this email to hit your inbox at 2 p.m. on Monday rather than 2 p.m. on Saturday."

4. **We avoid causing others to feel guilty for not working on the weekend.** As a whole, we educators are hard on ourselves and feel guilty for stepping away from work even on the weekends. When we see a lengthy, detailed, elaborate email from our boss or colleague hit our inbox on a Sunday morning, we tend to feel guilty for taking time for ourselves or our families. My self-care might be sneaking in a few hours to work on a weekend morning because I feel so far behind, but I certainly don't want my few hours of work to cause others to feel guilty about not working.

5. **We use technology tools that increase our efficiency.** Tools such as the Boomerang Chrome extension allow us to schedule our emails so if we do spend a little time working on the weekend, our emails can go out at the perfect time on Monday. Gmail has a feature that allows you to schedule emails to send later. If you're not tech savvy, you can draft your email on the weekend and then send it out early the next week.

6. **We remember that our emergency is not someone else's emergency.** I might wake up on a Saturday thinking, "Oh darn, I forgot to communicate such and such!" However, nine times out of ten, my emergency is not anyone else's emergency. I challenge myself to save up as many messages as I can throughout the week to include in our weekly staff update. Surprisingly, just about everything can wait a couple of days.

7. **We make Monday mornings more enjoyable.** Wouldn't it be wonderful to check your work email on Monday morning

to find a couple of messages rather than a flooded inbox? Easing our way slowly back into the workweek sounds lovely, doesn't it? I work hard to celebrate Mondays at least as much as I celebrate Fridays, and having a manageable inbox would greatly help the cause. If you would like to join me in avoiding sending group emails on the weekend, let's also vary the time we schedule our Monday emails so they hit inboxes throughout the day rather than all at once.

REDUCE THE WORRY LOAD

It's not just the workload causing educators to flee; it's the worry load, too.

One beautiful lesson from COVID-19 is that things can change on a dime. That means what is worrying me today may be a distant memory tomorrow—either because it gets resolved or because something more important takes its place. I have gotten really good at focusing on issues or problems that are right here, right now. I tell myself that I can worry about the nonpressing issues later. And somehow with the passage of time, most of those nonpressing issues become nonissues. I saw this quote from Kevin Miller the other day, and it stuck with me: "What you give your attention to owns you. Choose wisely."

Conceptually, choosing to worry later about some things is a great idea. Yet educators often struggle with this because they have huge hearts and want to make a difference. They also want to do things right, and they care deeply for their students. When we are navigating crises left and right, every problem seems enormous because we are overwhelmed and facing burnout.

So how do we reduce our worry load to feel less overwhelmed and stressed? Let's start by asking ourselves these three questions:

- **Are my feelings about this issue aligned with the size of the problem?** When we are struggling, all problems feel like big problems. Pausing to ask ourselves if our reaction to the situation matches the actual size of the problem can help us align our reactions appropriately and reduce the worry load we take on.

- **Is this my problem to solve or someone else's?** If you are like me, you may get all worked up about something that is not your problem to solve. If the problem is not within your control, recognize that you'd be better off letting it go. If it *is* your problem to solve, however, or if you might have influence over the outcome, choose action steps that help you productively reduce the amount of worry and stress you feel.

- **Is this a pressing issue right now, or can I postpone my worry about it?** Often we are bothered about things that change or resolve themselves before we actually need to worry about them. Or something bigger comes along that makes what we were worrying about seem like a mouse problem rather than a mammoth problem. Don't you feel like this is especially true now with things changing at such a fast pace? Sometimes I even give myself a worry date and put it on my calendar. I decide I can start worrying about this event two weeks before it begins, but for now, I let it go.

It's also helpful to remember that our windows of stress tolerance are almost filled with the everyday stuff we encounter. Things we used to tolerate pretty well can set us on edge when we have little room for all the additional stress a day will bring. Cut yourself some slack for feeling overwhelmed. Don't add guilt to the burdens you bear. In addition to giving yourself grace, see if there are any stressors you can let go of to create more space for the inevitable challenges of the day.

This unattributed quote about the 5×5 rule can help us decide what is really worth our worry: "If it won't matter in five years, don't spend more than five minutes worrying about it." When it comes down to it, we spend way too much time worrying about things that won't matter in five years.

IDEAS TO IMPLEMENT TOMORROW:

- Set up a staff Zen Zone either temporarily or permanently. It will speak volumes to your staff about how you prioritize their wellness.
- Reflect on your email practices and determine one action step you can take to reduce the email burden on your staff.
- Share a two-minute self-care tip with your staff in your next staff newsletter.
- Visit AllysonApsey.com to find a wellness blog post to share with your staff.
- Share your own ideas with the #LeadingtheWholeTeacher community on social media.

QUESTIONS FOR COLLABORATION AND REFLECTION:

- What email practices are you rethinking?
- Beth shared a teacher's perspective on self-care. What surprised you in her story? What changes are you considering?
- How might you help teachers reduce their worry load?

CHAPTER 7

GIVING TEACHERS A SEAT AT THE DECISION-MAKING TABLE

Teamwork requires some sacrifice up front; people who work as a team have to put the collective needs of the group ahead of their individual interests.

—Patrick Lencioni

Can you think of a single instance where teacher input wouldn't benefit the decision-making process regarding teaching and learning? No? Me neither. Gathering evidence and data to inform the decision, identifying various options, predicting barriers—every step of this process benefits from the input of those who will be implementing the decision. Yet these decisions are often made without teachers at the decision-making table.

In my experience, this is not an intentional oversight. I have worked with district leadership teams composed of really smart people who move thoughtfully through the decision-making process. They believe they are thoroughly vetting the options, getting input from stakeholders, and making the best decisions for the organization. However, these groups often include educators far removed from the implementation of the decisions—superintendents, assistant superintendents, and directors. There is just no way that individuals who will not be implementing a decision can think of all the variables. We need teachers at the table.

According to research, including a diverse group of stakeholders in the decision-making process leads to better decisions.[1] We also know through surveys that employees often feel left out of the decision-making process, and they pinpoint a lack of communication as a source of many issues in an organization.[2] If you are not yet convinced that teachers belong at the decision-making table, consider another truth, quoted from *Lead Like a Pirate: Make School Amazing for Your Students and Staff* by Shelley Burgess and Beth Houf: "People are less likely to tear down systems they help build."[3]

THE IDEA OF PRINCIPAL ESTIMATES OF TEACHER ACHIEVEMENT

So how do we invite a more diverse group—that includes teachers—to the decision-making process in education? First, we must *believe* that teachers belong at the table.

Fortunately, research serves as a compelling guide for which teacher and school practices have the biggest impact on student learning. We can all agree that time is a precious commodity during the school day and that it is important to maximize our efforts in the classroom to support student achievement. Let's talk about John Hattie's research on the effect size of classroom, home, and school influences. As we already know, effect size is used in research to determine the relationship between two things, and the larger the effect size, the better. Hattie determined

---

1 Katherine W. Phillips, "How Diversity Makes Us Smarter," *Scientific American,* October 1, 2014, scientificamerican.com/article/how-diversity-makes-us-smarter.

2 Lauren Landry, "Why Managers Should Involve Their Team in the Decision-Making Process," updated June 6, 2022, Harvard Business School Online's Business Insights (blog), online.hbs.edu/blog/post/team-decision-making.

3 Shelley Burgess and Beth Houf, *Lead Like a Pirate: Make School Amazing for Your Students and Staff* (San Diego: Dave Burgess Consulting, Inc., 2017), 23.

that the average effect size for all the interventions he studied was 0.4, which he called the *hinge point*. This means that interventions with an effect size greater than 0.4 are better than average. Teacher estimates of student achievement has an effect size of 1.29, which indicates that it is a powerful tool.[4]

I think about teacher estimates of student achievement often—when I'm driving, when I'm in the shower, as I try to sleep at night. I know, I know, exciting life, eh? Before I tell you why teacher estimates of student achievement has been on my mind, let's define what we mean by this. A teacher estimate of achievement is the teacher's belief about the level a student is able to achieve based on past experiences.

To not only have high expectations for students but to *know* they are capable of achieving great things, teachers need strong, positive relationships with their students. Before any learning can happen, students need to feel safe and valued. Once trusting relationships are established, teachers can communicate that they know their students are capable of great things.

To paraphrase *Field of Dreams*, "If you build it, they will come."

OK, we understand Hattie's research on effect size and what it means, and now we understand what "teacher estimates of achievement" means. True confession: as I was thinking about Hattie's research in relation to estimates of achievement, I wasn't only thinking about students. I was also thinking about teachers.

I've wondered whether principal estimates of teacher achievement would have the same effect size on teacher learning. Would that translate into a similar positive impact on student achievement?

School leaders, do you believe in your teachers' capacity? Can I request a sidebar? I have an aversion to using the word *capacity* when talking about teachers. If we think our job as leaders is to build capacity in teachers, then are we saying they don't already *have* the capacity? What if we instead believe that every single teacher not only has the

---

4 Hattie, *Visible Learning*.

capacity to learn and grow in their practice but that they want to learn and grow? Would that increase principal estimates of teacher achievement and in turn positively impact student achievement? Teachers have the capacity to learn, grow, and implement research-proven practices, and when leaders believe that, the sky's the limit.

I have so many hopeful questions about this idea.

If teachers don't *know* that every one of their students has the capacity and ability to learn, to strengthen their skills, to achieve amazing things, what business do these teachers have in the classroom?

If principals don't *know* that every one of the teachers in their school has the capacity and ability to learn best practices, to strengthen their skills, to do amazing things for students, what business do those principals have leading them?

I cannot help but wonder how this shift in thinking could impact teacher evaluation. Is this shift needed as we work to transform teacher evaluation from something scary and divisive to something that can help strengthen relationships and propel teachers toward their goals?

How could this shift in thinking impact relationships between principals and teachers?

How could removing fear from the environment and replacing it with empowerment impact collegial relationships? Teacher-student relationships? How could it transform the school culture?

Would *knowing* that teachers have the knowledge and ability to contribute to important decisions mean inviting them to the decision-making table more often? School leaders who believe that including diverse perspectives leads to better decisions will not only have better outcomes—they will also have more engaged and satisfied teachers.

THE MANY ROLES IN THE DECISION-MAKING PROCESS

Time can feel like the enemy when making decisions, and it can sometimes be the culprit behind a lack of collaboration in the decision process. The other enemies of collaborative decisions include the perception that only a few people have adequate background knowledge about the decisions and only those few people understand the complexity of the problem. These issues will all understandably pop up, which is why it's important to recognize the many key parts of the decision-making process.

Identify and analyze the problem.

Getting boots-on-the-ground input when making decisions is important and empowering to teachers, and it can absolutely result in more comprehensive and better decisions. For instance, when selecting a curriculum tool, it is important to use a process that allows teachers to identify the challenges with the current tools, address the gaps in student-learning needs, share how ease of use and functionality impact learning, etc. This input can be collected through a carefully crafted survey or, even better, through collaborative discussions with teachers who will bring various perspectives to the table.

Vet and pilot options.

Involving teachers in vetting options and piloting new ideas or programs is beneficial for many reasons. First, teachers can give important implementation input that should be considered with each option. Second, teachers value other teachers' recommendations; the recommendation of a respected teacher leader heavily outweighs a central office recommendation. The entire change process has the potential to run much smoother with the involvement of teachers. Remember that it is important to include teachers with diverse perspectives to gain the maximum benefit.

Determine implementation barriers.

Even if for some reason a district or school cannot invite teachers to participate in the decision-making process, it is important to invite them to help identify implementation barriers. For instance, if a time crunch means teachers can only help assess a new ELA curriculum tool through survey results, at the minimum it is important to gather a group of teachers (with diverse perspectives—see a pattern here?) to help determine what barriers may interfere with implementation of the tool. Leaders can then create an action plan to help reduce the barriers and maximize communication.

THE WEEKLY STAFF CHECK-IN

I discovered a great communication tool during a meeting with our teachers. One of the teachers was telling us about the benefits of doing a systematic check-in with students after recess. The process is simple: students use a slip of paper to indicate whether recess was without problems, whether they had a problem but solved it, or whether they had a problem they needed help solving. This little check-in helps the teacher support their students, reinforces the idea that the students are capable of solving problems, and preserves precious learning time.

As we discussed the value of routine check-ins with students, the idea of routine check-ins with staff members came up. Genius! I jumped on the idea and created a weekly staff check-in to start using the next week. After talking with teachers about the concept, they suggested we keep it as easy as possible. They also sweetly warned that if I was going to ask the question, I needed to be ready for the answers. Here is the check-in I sent out that first Monday.

I've invited you to fill out a form:

Monday Morning Staff Check-In

How are you feeling about the week ahead?
- O   I am doing great, looking forward to the week!
- O   I have lots of work to do, but I am going to be okay.
- O   I am overwhelmed and need some extra TLC.
- O   HELP me! I could really use some help with something. (Please comment in "Other" what you could use help with.)
- O   Other: _____

To be honest, I read the first results with one eye open. As expected, the responses were a mixed bag, with some staff members feeling great, some with simple questions, and others feeling completely overwhelmed and wanting help. I knew it was important for me to do something with the information, so I made sure the form would collect email addresses so I could answer questions and provide the support requested immediately. I was also thankful that our staff felt comfortable enough to give genuine responses.

The question-and-answer selections have changed over the years to address specific needs and keep it fresh. For example, during remote learning at the beginning of the COVID-19 pandemic, we changed the survey to better represent the challenges of being at home.

I've invited you to fill out a form:

Monday Morning Staff Check-In (COVID-19 Edition)

How are you feeling about the week ahead?

- ○ We are doing well. I feel good about our plan for the week
- ○ We are doing okay, thankful we are not sick.
- ○ We have sick family members, but we are doing okay.
- ○ Please call me, I need some TLC.
- ○ Please tag me in to remotely work on a project, I am going stir-crazy.
- ○ I would love to connect virtually to learn together (book study, etc.).
- ○ I am not doing well at all, either physically or emotionally, and would love some help.
- ○ Other: _____

After several years of this practice, I cannot imagine ever discontinuing it. Not only is it a quick and easy way for teachers to communicate with me about the week ahead, but it also nurtures our relationships and models what we are asking teachers to do with their students. We may edit the questions as we move along, but this systematic communication tool has proved to be priceless.

Regular, frequent communication with teachers is an essential part of giving them a seat at the decision-making table. If school leaders know what challenges teachers face, teachers will be more apt to turn to them to help identify the roots of a problem and brainstorm potential solutions. But the weekly check-in survey is not a catchall. Some staff prefer face-to-face check-ins or the ability to shoot their leader an email or text when something is on their mind. However, systematic check-ins help build the culture of reciprocal communication that can open the door to honest and ongoing conversations. As Rollo May wrote, "Communication leads to community, that is, to understanding, intimacy, and mutual valuing." A variety of communication methods is necessary to build a positive, trusting school community.

IDEAS TO IMPLEMENT TOMORROW:

- Reflect on the decision-making process in your school or district. Are teachers regularly given seats at the table where final decisions are made? What is an area for growth in your district or school?

- Consider implementing a weekly check-in for your staff. Brainstorm what question you might ask them and what answer choices you could give. Check out AllysonApsey.com to see a system for regular follow-up to the check-in. (Search for the COVID-19 weekly check-in post.)

- As you read the section on principal estimates of teacher achievement, did any of your staff members come to mind? Take a couple of minutes to reflect on how you might change the script in your head about that staff member.

- Share your ideas about inviting teachers to the decision-making table using #LeadingtheWholeTeacher on social media.

QUESTIONS FOR COLLABORATION AND REFLECTION:

- What is a teacher collaboration strength at your school? What might be your next step?

- Can you think of a time when teachers weren't invited to the decision-making table and implementation suffered because of it? How might this be remedied?

- Thinking back on your own experiences, what are some benefits of increasing principal estimates of teacher achievement?

CHAPTER 8

FOSTERING CONTINUOUS EDUCATOR GROWTH

Live as if you were to die tomorrow. Learn as if you were to live forever.

—Mahatma Gandhi

Fostering continuous growth for educators is the last of the six pillars of the whole teacher, and it comes last for a reason. The other components of the whole teacher need to be in place before teachers can open themselves up to the risks that come with reflecting and changing. When we feel strong and powerful, we are ready to learn, grow, and conquer the world. One of the many reasons it is important to serve the whole teacher in our schools is so they feel strong enough to seek continuous growth. When we feel weak, defeated, and powerless, even the smallest changes and challenges can seem insurmountable.

Educators have servant hearts, and they desire to continuously improve so they can serve their students better. The word *better* is tricky because we often think that seeking improvement means we're doing something wrong. But that is just not true. The reality is that we never stay stagnant—we are always improving or declining. The process of continuous improvement is a reward unto itself; learning can be deeply fulfilling, especially when the learning is self-selected and an area of passion. Carl Friedrich Gauss teaches us that "it is not knowledge, but the act of learning, not possession but the act of getting there, which grants the greatest enjoyment."

Learning and growing can be very need satisfying. Let's think back to Glasser's five basic needs of love and belonging, freedom, power, fun, and survival. What need(s) do you think learning can help us meet? Glasser taught us that learning is a great way to help us meet our need for power, and this is true for students and for educators. Teachers often talk about how they love the lightbulb moments with students. Picture students' faces during those lightbulb moments. What feeling does their expression evoke? They feel joy, excitement, or even surprise. That is true learning. How often do teachers get to experience that for themselves? Not often enough, if ever.

In chapter 2 we learned that Glasser said authentic learning experiences can also help us meet our need for fun. Sometimes learning can help us meet our need for freedom as well, especially when there is choice involved in learning. Choice can be incorporated in what we learn, the resources we explore to do the learning, and how we share our learning. Let's look at some ways we can support teachers in deep, authentic learning and empower continuous growth.

STAFF COLLABORATION TIME

What others might call "staff meetings" we call "staff collaboration time," and this simple switch has made a huge difference. We know now that when we gather as a staff everyone will be contributing to our learning, and this concept lends itself perfectly to the idea of fostering continuous growth. If an issue doesn't involve some component of collaboration, it doesn't belong in our meeting time. And just as with decision-making, there can always be space for teacher collaboration when we get together.

The adage "If it could be an email, it shouldn't be a meeting" is mostly true. Yet there are occasions when disseminating information in person is better than emailing, like when the information may cause big emotions or confusion. The opportunity to ask questions and seek clarification in the group setting is in itself collaboration.

Having a culture of collaboration in a school or district means having a culture where everyone is expected to learn, grow, and contribute. It means that everyone's voice and perspective is valued. Changing the name of your staff meetings can be a good start to developing that culture.

TEACHER GENIUS HOUR

Teachers are often asked to set goals for the year, and giving them freedom to select a goal tied to a passion can set the stage for an authentic learning experience. This same opportunity is sometimes provided for students through a Genius Hour in which they choose a topic they want to learn about and decide how they will teach it to their classmates. Wouldn't it be great to provide that to teachers as well? And it would be a terrific bonus if they could use it as a goal to fulfill a teacher evaluation requirement.

Teachers may want to explore classroom management systems that empower students, ideas to increase student response rates, or how to confer with students about their self-selected independent reading books. Leaders can support teacher learning by providing access to resources, learning alongside teachers, and/or providing time for teachers to learn about their area of passion.

Teachers could share their learning at staff meetings or through breakout presentations for their colleagues. This idea is a triple win—it has the potential to significantly impact students in positive ways, it can increase teacher leadership in the school, and it fosters a culture of continuous improvement.

SUMMER LEARNING

We all know that although the pace slows down, educators do not really have summers "off." Instead, teachers dream about the new school year, plan lessons, set up their classrooms, and attend professional development. But because the pace is slower, they are often interested in learning over the summer. One way to support this is to ask them what they want to learn about and then match their interests with PD offerings and/or book studies. Sending a survey out a month before the break can give leaders time to provide summer learning support. Here is an example of a survey I've used, though you might want to use one that is more open-ended.

Hello Q-Crew,

As we dream about next year, I am wondering if you would be interested in doing some summer learning in small groups together. This would be totally optional and could be little book studies, finding webinars/videos to share, etc. If you are remotely interested in any of the topics below, could you check that box and submit this form? Also, if you have another idea, please add that. Your colleagues would, likely be interested in that topic too. Thank you! Allyson

This summer, I dream of learning about:

- O   Restorative Practice
- O   Inclusion, Diversity, Equity and Access
- O   Math Workshop
- O   Writing Workshop
- O   Other: _____

Be sure to note in the survey that summer learning is optional. I wanted to support my teachers in their efforts to grow and learn, yet I did not want those who weren't interested to feel guilty at all. It is important to protect summer as a time of freedom, renewal, and rest for educators.

Remote learning options make it easier now to match teacher passions with professional learning opportunities. While there are advantages to connecting remotely with educators from across the country or the world, tapping into PD offerings in your area is wonderful for networking in person. Leaders can help teachers find PD offerings by connecting with education organizations and educational leaders through social media.

COLLECTIVE EFFICACY

We know that teachers working together to achieve goals benefits student learning and contributes to strong, positive relationships among school staff. This also contributes to their continuous growth as professionals. Teaching teams, professional learning communities, and practices like instructional rounds can be helpful for continuous growth.

It takes concerted effort from school leaders to create opportunities for developing collective teacher efficacy. For example, you can schedule shared planning time for teacher teams. The teams will benefit from guidance as they create their collective commitments to work together, and frequent check-ins from school leaders help to support them in these shared goals.

IDEAS TO IMPLEMENT TOMORROW:

- Reflect on where authentic learning (or lightbulb moments) happen for teachers in your school or district. What is an area of strength?
- Survey your teachers to find out their areas of passion and match them with each other to share what they know and what they want to learn. Then support them with resources and ideas that you gather.
- Consider how renaming your staff meetings could support a culture of continuous learning and growth.

- We want to learn from you! Share your ideas about fostering continuous educator growth using #LeadingtheWholeTeacher on social media.

QUESTIONS FOR COLLABORATION AND REFLECTION:

- Think back to a time when you experienced a positive challenge at work. What were the circumstances that set you up for that important learning moment? How might they be replicated at your school?

- How might you incorporate choice in learning for teachers in your school or district?

- What is your main takeaway regarding how to support collective teacher efficacy? How might you maximize time for professional learning or shared planning in your school?

CHAPTER 9

LEADING THE WHOLE TEACHER THROUGH CRISIS

Life is a storm, my young friend. You will bask in the sunlight one moment, be shattered on the rocks the next. What makes you a man is what you do when that storm comes. You must look into that storm and shout....Do your worst, for I will do mine!

—Alexandre Dumas

If you're looking for an expert in leading through crisis, you may want to look elsewhere. I am a school leader who is learning every day how to lead through crisis, just like so many educators out there. In my nearly twenty years as a principal, I did occasionally experience crises before COVID-19, but those crises were different. They would come, rock our worlds, teach us a whole lot, and then go away. Those crises had an end. In contrast, COVID-19 was one long crisis that morphed and flowed and sometimes appeared to be ending, but that's just to give us an ember of hope to keep us going.

The pandemic wreaked havoc on our schools and multiplied the problems we already faced in education. Before the pandemic, we were lobbying for help with staff shortages, and now we have shortages in every area: teachers, support staff, bus drivers, childcare providers, recess supervisors, custodial staff. You name it, we are short staffed.

Before the pandemic, we were working to become trauma-informed educators because of skyrocketing social-emotional needs in our schools. Now the number of students who struggle with regulating their behavior is at an all-time high. And remember those staff shortages I mentioned? We know there are no additional staff to help the kids who are struggling.

With substitute teachers in short supply and high demand, teachers cannot even take a day off in peace because they have no idea who will be covering their classrooms. By the way, bless you to the few angels who are subbing for our schools. We are so thankful for you!

Educators are fleeing the profession in record numbers because it is so hard. Teachers are leaving, principals are leaving, support staff are leaving, and there is no one coming to replace them.

OK, so this is where I'm supposed to say that not all hope is lost. So I will.

Not all hope is lost.

You know why? Because educators are talented, passionate, and servant-hearted, and we *will not give up* on our people or our students. We won't even give up on the parents who are so mad at us that we're covered with their spittle after they finish yelling at us about things we cannot control. We won't give up on anyone.

I repeat: I am not an expert in leading through crises. I am, however, committed to becoming a better leader because of crises. I renew that commitment every day while I'm getting ready for school. I have a personal mantra that I repeat as necessary to help me be the best leader I can be—even when facing challenges I have never experienced before:

I will get out of my own way

and be the leader you need today.

I will not let fear run this school;

I will run this school.

I get to serve my school community
and that is a blessing.

If you are a teacher reading this book, just replace "school" with "classroom." And thank you for reading a book that can help you recognize how to meet your own needs and support colleagues in doing the same.

We learned so much while we navigated the years of the COVID-19 crisis, and I've remained determined to learn and grow as a leader regardless of the challenges that come my way. As I was reflecting on all I've learned, I created this to-do list for leading during crises.

Remember that everything we do matters a hundred times more during a crisis.

When I became a principal, I had no clue that every single little thing I do matters. I didn't understand that I could ruin trust and relationships with an offhand comment to someone. People watch their leaders—their body language, what they do and what they don't do—and they listen carefully. They look to their leaders to see how they should feel about things and to determine the magnitude of a situation. Gosh, maybe it was good that I didn't know the enormous responsibility of being a leader because I might have run in the other direction. During a crisis, leaders are watched like hawks, and everything we do matters even more.

By leaders, I don't just mean principals. Teachers are leaders for their students, their students' families, and their colleagues. Anyone who looks out for the good of others is a leader in some capacity, and that includes all school staff: support staff, food service staff, bus drivers, etc. For all of us, what we do matters a hundred times more during a crisis because people are seeking information from our actions, our words, and even what we choose to be silent about. No pressure, right?

Listen more than ever.

I love the advice from Michael Bungay Stanier on an episode of Brené Brown's *Dare to Lead* podcast called "The Advice Trap and Staying Curious Just a Little Longer."[1] Michael is the author of the best-selling book *The Coaching Habit: Say Less, Ask More & Change the Way You Lead Forever.* On the podcast, he shared so many nuggets of wisdom that have stuck with me, but when he talked about "staying curious a little longer," I felt it deep in my soul. During a crisis, so many things come at leaders at once that we might be tempted to solve problems as quickly as possible. I think of that Whac-A-Mole game at arcades: we want to whack those pesky mole problems as quickly as possible because we know another one will be popping up immediately. Instead, during a crisis, we need to slow down and listen.

This is a time to avoid multitasking as much as possible so you can give your whole attention to the person (or task) in front of you. This quote by Jeremy Clarkson, broadcaster, journalist, game show host, and writer, rings true to me: "Multitasking is the ability to screw everything up simultaneously." Relationships are the last things we want to screw up during a crisis, so close the laptop and ignore the smartwatch notifications and really, really listen. The only way to give your whole attention to someone is to eliminate other distractions, and when we really listen, we avoid solving problems so quickly that we end up creating more problems.

Empathize.

I like sunshine and rainbows, and my strong inclination is to get everything back to that state as quickly as possible. Sometimes this means I don't allow myself or others to sit in negative emotions long enough. But sometimes things just suck. Period. It is extremely important to feel

---

1 Brené Brown, "The Advice Trap and Staying Curious Just a Little Longer with Michael Bungay Stanier," April 26, 2021, *Dare to Lead*, podcast, Spotify, 1:08:24, brenebrown.com/podcast/brene-with-michael-bungay-stanier-on-the-advice -trap-and-staying-curious-just-a-little-longer/.

with people during times of crisis because that is how we connect at a deep level. Celebrate big when good things happen. Cry together when bad things happen. It is amazing how connecting through emotions helps us feel supported by our leaders.

I never understood jeans days in schools because I didn't understand why teachers couldn't wear jeans whenever they wanted. So we took advantage of the opportunity COVID-19 presented us to do things differently and gave out a "jeans pass" to teachers, saying that if we have to wear masks every day, we can also wear jeans every day. This bit of freedom helped us overcome some of the other challenges we were facing.

To support teachers in understanding the grace we all needed to give each other to get through the crisis, we also handed out "get out of jail free" cards (like the Monopoly game cards) as necessary. For example, if you snap at a colleague or have big emotions about something that isn't so big, you can hand a card to your colleague to ask for grace. This little tool served as a reminder that we're all human and make mistakes—and that we all deserve grace.

Remember that people are people first.

Recognizing that students, staff, and families are people first helps leaders focus on basic needs above all else. During a crisis, our people are scared, stressed, and sensitive, and they are sick of the current situation. They have issues at home on top of all the issues at school. They may break down, take things personally, and be full of self-doubt. Knowing their leader values their health above all and sees them as whole people can help them put on a brave face and come to work with renewed hope every morning. It also helps them support their colleagues in the same way.

Communicate, communicate, communicate.

As I've said, with a lack of information, our minds go to negative places. During a crisis especially, with all the negative stuff out there, we need to clearly communicate to a fault so we don't make up more negative stuff in our heads. Now, I do not mean that we should send ten emails a day (refer to the email tips in chapter 6 as necessary). Nobody wants that. But during times of emotional duress and crisis, information needs to be easy to access. Leaders also need to be easy to access. Make yourself easy to access by getting into as many classrooms as possible every day. Do a weekly check-in with staff so they can let you know what they need.

Add in a plus-one.

A plus-one is an additional message we build into communication, and it is especially important to utilize this strategy during times of crisis. For example, when we have a message to share—maybe about a half day that's coming up—the plus-one is an extra message that helps build relationships and strengthen your school culture. To remind families of the half day and add in a plus-one, we could write an email like this:

> **Dear Families,**
>
> **You get to start the weekend early with a half day this Friday. We are having an amazing week and we are sorry to cut it a little short, but we look forward to seeing all your smiling faces on Monday morning.**
>
> **Thank you!**
> **Your Grateful School Staff**

After practicing the plus-one strategy for a while now, I find myself typing a quick email and then hesitating when I go to press Send. In that pause, I ask myself where I could build in a plus-one statement that will help build a relationship or where I could add something that would make the recipient's day. How could I enhance our culture in addition to communicating the intended message? Adding a message to build up staff and/or our community is especially important during fragile times of crisis. We need to take advantage of every opportunity to strengthen our schools when it can feel like there are outside forces working to weaken us.

Adding a plus-one is valuable for a couple of reasons. First, even if the original purpose of the communication is misconstrued, the plus-one usually isn't misunderstood. Therefore, communication is never wasted because it always helps build relationships or culture. Also, it is hard to interpret a message in a negative way when we are deliberately adding in positivity. So many times the media or other sources try to tell our story for us during a crisis. Leaders need to grab hold of any opportunity to be their own storytellers.

Second, the plus-one helps slide relationship-building and culture-building messages into our everyday communication, and this becomes a way of life for us. For example, I might email staff to remind them of something mundane like a meeting location but slip in the fact that I love them or that they are amazing. Two birds, one stone. Letting staff know that we are still the same loving, supportive school is crucial during a crisis because emotions are running high and patience is running low.

If we can add a plus-one to quick emails or even our voice mail messages, where else could we add one in? Smiling and expressing gratitude as often as possible is an easy way to add a plus-one in face-to-face communication. Could we add a plus-one into a math lesson? An intercom announcement? You betcha! We can slide in a plus-one anywhere. My favorite place to slide in a plus-one is in my voice mail message: "Hello, you've reached Allyson Apsey, the luckiest principal in the world. Please leave a message . . ."

Play!

Remember how I said that people watch leaders like a hawk during crisis? If you are worried all the time, they will be worried all the time. If you spend time playing and laughing each day, they will spend time playing and laughing each day. Like I mentioned earlier, at the beginning of the COVID-19 pandemic, I felt that it would be ridiculous for me to put on wigs, dance with my fanny pack with speakers, or make silly videos when we were just trying to keep everyone healthy. I am embarrassed to say that it took me a couple of months to realize that the opposite was true—it was ridiculous that I was allowing the pandemic to rob us of joy and play.

Laughter reduces stress, relaxes muscles, and builds relationships. Not only should we play and laugh during a crisis, but we should also do it more frequently than ever. During a crisis, ideas like weekly Movement Mondays (when we wear workout clothes and have fun moving with our students) and monthly Wonderful Wednesdays (when staff share treats and connect) are more important than ever. Another way we promote play and fun at our school is by choosing an upbeat theme song every year, such as Katy Perry's "Electric" or Meghan Trainor's "Better When I'm Dancing," that helps reinforce our joyful environment.

IDEAS TO IMPLEMENT TOMORROW:

- A school culture that serves the whole teacher sets your staff up for working through any challenge that comes their way. What is one whole-teacher practice you will put in place that will also serve your school community during a crisis?
- Choose one mode of communication that you will add a plus-one to. You could start with your voice mail message or your email signature.
- Consider selecting a theme song to help your school culture for the remainder of this school year or next school year. What feelings do you want the song to evoke? Check out

AllysonApsey.com for a list of the theme songs we used at Quincy Elementary.

- Could you have a jeans day every day? What would that mean to your teachers?
- We want to learn from you! Share your ideas about leading through crisis using #LeadingtheWholeTeacher on social media.

QUESTIONS FOR COLLABORATION AND REFLECTION:

- When you led through a crisis, what did you learn? How has it transformed your leadership?

- What did you connect most with in this chapter about leading through crisis?

- Play is such an important element in school. How might you implement more play throughout the school day and school year?

CHAPTER 10

FOCUSING ON
PERSONAL WELLNESS

Keep good company, read good books, love good things and cultivate soul and body as faithfully as you can.

—Louisa May Alcott

The perfect concluding chapter for a book focused on taking care of the whole teacher is a call to action to take care of yourself. There's a quote by Sam Levenson that I love. He writes, "As you grow older, you will discover you have two hands: one for helping yourself, the other for helping others." It is just as important to take care of your whole self as it is to care for others.

The focus on self-care over the past few years has left many of us inspired to take better care of ourselves, which is exactly the point. That's wonderful. But like Beth Joselyn told us, some have felt like the talk about self-care has missed the mark and the pressure to do it has inadvertently created anxiety and guilt. To others, it has felt like a very privileged concept. As people struggle to put food on the table, take care of their families, and balance work and home responsibilities, are they supposed to drop everything and take a bubble bath? It just doesn't mesh with reality, and adding pressure and stress to our lives is the last thing the idea of self-care was intended to do.

Let's shift our thinking from self-care to personal wellness to bridge that gap and encompass the intended concept of putting the oxygen mask on ourselves first. Rather than adding self-care to our daily or weekly to-do list, let's focus on listening to our hearts, our bodies, and our spirits more carefully and then acting upon that information. Taking care of ourselves amid our daily grind could help us and those around us as well. The Dalai Lama said it so well: "If you feel 'burnout' setting in, if you feel demoralized and exhausted, it is best, for the sake of everyone, to withdraw and restore yourself."

TAKE A WELLNESS PAUSE

It doesn't take a global pandemic or crisis to feel like our emotions are determined by what is happening in the world around us. Stress and challenges will always be part of our daily lives. Sometimes we feel like our job is to avoid negative emotions, but we will always fail in that endeavor. Rather than setting ourselves up for failure, let's build in practices that will help us manage negative emotions so they don't manage us. While personal wellness encompasses exercise, eating right, and getting enough sleep, it also means being a good self-listener to understand what our own emotions are telling us. One way to practice this is to take a wellness pause.

When we feel angry, sad, overwhelmed, jealous, or another negative emotion, we feel that way for a reason. Our body, mind, heart, or spirit is trying to tell us something. There is no guilt or shame in having negative emotions; we all experience them because we are supposed to. They have a purpose. Pausing may help us work through the negative emotions and move toward personal wellness. Below is a graphic I created to help illustrate this process. A pentagon illustrates that there are five things we may need to help us move into a more effective space. Inside the pentagon are three questions we can ask ourselves or one another to help us take advantage of a tool that may help us feel better.

TAKE A WELLNESS PAUSE...

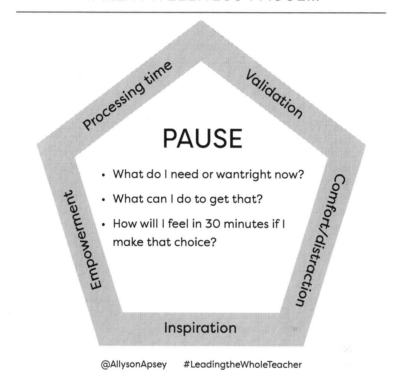

@AllysonApsey   #LeadingtheWholeTeacher

We can take a wellness pause by stopping what we are doing and taking a moment to breathe. Slowing down our breath and paying attention to it, we can take as long as we need until we are ready to answer these three questions.

What do I need or want right now? This question may be the most important. At this moment, what do you want or need? Do you need validation of your feelings? Do you need empowerment? Do you need processing time? Do you need comfort or distraction? Do you need inspiration?

As you can see in the graphic, these answers are listed on the sides of the pentagon: processing time, validation, comfort/distraction, inspiration, and empowerment. You may need or want more than one. Sometimes we need someone to validate our feelings, to acknowledge that what we're going through is hard and we are not crazy to feel that way. Sometimes we need to sit in our negative feelings and process them. Sometimes we need someone to inspire us to snap out of the negativity and focus on the positive. These answers are OK, and they give us valuable information as we move on to the next question.

What can I do to get that? If you are like me, you call specific people for specific reasons. For example, it's risky to call my husband when I want my feelings validated because he tends to go right into problem-solving mode. If I want comfort and distraction, I call friends who will make me laugh no matter what. One thing to consider as we decide how we can get what we want or need is that the only person we can control is ourselves. If I call a friend looking for inspiration but she's had a terrible day and has nothing to give me, I might leave that conversation feeling worse. If I am not feeling strong enough to take that risk, my solution needs to depend only on me. In that case, if I decide I need comfort and distraction, watching HGTV usually does the trick. If I need empowerment, exercising almost always helps. When I identify that what I really need is processing time, I may find an environment that is soothing to me, like the woods or a moment in the sunshine, and take a pause to connect to my feelings. Or I might journal or blog to help me process.

A good way to motivate ourselves to take the next step and act upon our answer is to ask ourselves the third question.

How will I feel in thirty minutes if I make that choice? An excellent path to action is to picture how we will feel after we make a choice. This question not only motivates us but is also empowering because it implies that our feelings are within our control. We cannot crinkle our noses like Jeannie in *I Dream of Jeannie* and automatically feel better, but we can take action that will move us toward emotional regulation and personal wellness. To get started, consider how you might feel in thirty minutes if you take some time to write and reflect. Or ask yourself another question: "How will I feel in thirty minutes if I don't listen to what I need right now?"

USE THE WELLNESS PAUSE TO HELP OTHERS

The three questions in the wellness pause are important to ask ourselves, but they can also be helpful when someone calls us for help. In her "The Power of Vulnerability" TED Talk, Brené Brown spoke about empathy versus sympathy and gave great advice. She suggested that when someone calls you for help, the first thing to say is this: "I am so glad you told me."[1] Following that with the three questions from the wellness pause will help you support your friend, colleague, or family member in the way they need and want support. Using the five answers on the sides of the pentagon will help them identify what they want or need and how you can help.

I have nothing against spa days, bubble baths, or other forms of pampering. They just aren't the path to personal wellness. J. Stanford said, "Health is a state of body. Wellness is a state of being." Putting on your oxygen mask comes from self-listening and then taking action based on what you learn. Taking care of ourselves isn't something to add to our to-do list; instead, it is having the tools to regulate our emotions and get unstuck so we can move toward personal wellness. So often what holds us back isn't the world around us but our own creation. Managing our negative emotions keeps us from becoming our own stumbling block. Taking good care of ourselves is key to not only living our best lives but to supporting the people we love in the way they deserve.

---

1 Brown, "The Power of Vulnerability."

IDEAS TO IMPLEMENT TOMORROW:

- Practice taking a wellness pause when you are not in crisis mode. Having the practice under your belt will help you remember to take the pause the next time you are under stress.
- Share the wellness pause concept with a colleague, friend, or family member. You can visit AllysonApsey.com and search for "wellness pause" to find a link to send via email or text.
- Print out the wellness pause graphic and hang it where you will likely be when you're feeling stressed or frustrated. Visit AllysonApsey.com to find an easy-to-print version.
- Share your tips for personal wellness with our #LeadingtheWholeTeacher community on social media.

QUESTIONS FOR COLLABORATION AND REFLECTION:

- What ideas did this chapter generate for you about taking better care of yourself?
- What is your favorite way to pamper yourself when times get tough?
- Which part of the wellness pause did you most connect with? How might this practice fit into your personal wellness routine?

FINAL THOUGHTS

In every ending, there is a new beginning.

—Deborah Harkness

A s we move forward to create schools that support the whole teacher, let's spend a few minutes thinking through the six pillars of the whole teacher and the exciting plans we developed to help teachers feel a deep sense of value and meaning in their daily work.

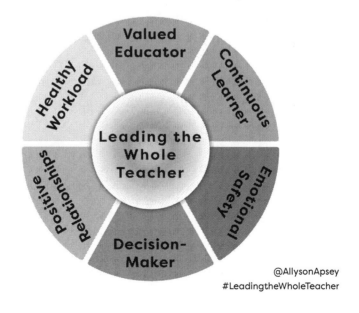

@AllysonApsey
#LeadingtheWholeTeacher

- **Emotional safety.** This pillar comes first because nothing else can happen until educators feel emotionally safe at school. To feel emotionally safe, teachers need to feel free from judgment, gossip, and criticism. They need to feel listened to and know it is safe to have emotions and take risks.

- **Valued educator.** Utilizing teacher evaluation as an empowerment tool is a great step in helping teachers feel valued and seen. The 10:1 rule applies to adults just as much as it applies to children. Educators need ten positives for every one negative. It is imperative that leaders recognize teachers' strengths to make them feel valued.

- **Positive relationships.** We build strong, healthy relationships when we feel strong and positive, so this pillar appropriately comes after emotional safety and feeling valued. Open, honest, and trusting relationships are the core of a positive and healthy school culture. We shared ideas for making this happen through self-awareness, sharing values, resolving conflict, and socializing.

- **Healthy workload.** Educators must stop wearing overworking like it's a badge of honor. The definition of a healthy workload varies from teacher to teacher, but there are three hallmarks of a healthy workload: feeling like working evenings or on weekends is a choice, having space for creativity, and feeling in control of your time during the school day. Leaders can protect healthy workloads by removing responsibilities from teachers' plates when possible and encouraging them to hold family and personal time sacred. Using email to inspire instead of baffle teachers can be a great place for leaders to start.

- **Decision-maker.** Teachers have a vast amount of knowledge, and so often they feel like decisions are made without their input. Or worse, they are asked for their input and then it is ignored. An important part of leading the whole teacher is to give them a seat at the decision-making table. Empowering their voices at any stage of the decision-making process will make for better decisions and implementation.

- **Continuous learner.** Teachers are hungry to grow and learn, but they are discouraged by the pendulum swing of initiatives in education. We can foster continuous growth and learning for teachers throughout the course of their careers by asking them how they learn best and what they would like to learn. Helping them seek continuous growth sparks creativity and reconnects them to their *why*.

It is time, my friends, to go forth and lead the whole teacher. Whether you're a school leader, a district leader, or a teacher working to lead yourself in a positive direction, you have all the tools you require to fulfill your needs at school and perform at your highest level. Our profession is better because you are in it—that is evidenced by your desire to continuously improve. Give yourself a little pat on the back for making it all the way to the end of this book. I even have a certificate for you if you complete the form on AllysonApsey.com to get the *Leading the Whole Teacher* endorsement.

Here's how we can keep the conversation going:

- Let's be friends! Please consider finding me on your favorite social media app so we can stay connected. Just look for Allyson Apsey on Twitter, Facebook, Instagram, etc. I am excited to learn from you.
- Email me (AllysonApsey@gmail.com) with questions or ideas you have—or if you'd like me to provide professional development about supporting the whole teacher.
- Please continue to share your amazing ideas about leading the whole teacher or personal wellness using #LeadingtheWholeTeacher on social media.
- Don't forget to visit AllysonApsey.com to complete the form to get your *Leading the Whole Teacher* endorsement.

ACKNOWLEDGMENTS

I am such a lucky girl. I have so many wise and inspiring friends, family members, and colleagues who help me continuously learn and grow. There are too many influences to name, but I would like to call out three special people who helped this book come to life. First, Cheryl Kraker is a friend and colleague who is a constant cheerleader, and I am not sure what I would do without her encouragement. Second, author and principal Brad Gustafson is always willing to take the time to give me authentic and thorough feedback on my writing, and I am forever grateful for him. Third, Beth Joselyn's perspective adds so much to this book, and I am proud of her for sharing her wisdom. We are all better for it.

Additionally, I'd like to thank my publisher, DBC Inc., and especially Shelley Burgess. Your friendship and your belief in me and in *Leading the Whole Teacher* is so appreciated. Thank you.

ABOUT THE AUTHOR

Allyson Apsey is an educational leader focused on creating need-satisfying school environments for students and staff where they feel seen and valued, and where they can thrive. She taught grades three through eight before becoming an award-winning school leader. Allyson has served as a principal for all levels K–12, as a state leader on the executive board of the Michigan Elementary and Middle School Principals Association (MEMSPA), and as a district leadership coach.

Allyson writes a blog called Serendipity in Education and has authored several books: *Leading the Whole Teacher*, *The Path to Serendipity: Discover the Gifts along Life's Journey*, *Through the Lens of Serendipity: Helping Others Discover the Best in Themselves—Even If Life Has Shown Them Its Worst*, the picture book *The Princes of Serendip*, and a middle-grade chapter book called *The Serendipity Journal*.

She has been published in *Principal* magazine and was featured in a TEDx Talk called "Serendipity Is Everywhere."

Allyson is an associate with Creative Leadership Solutions, where she works with districts and schools across the nation to improve performance at every level, from the classroom to the boardroom, with evidence, passion, and results. She also travels to spread her #SerendipityEDU message across the country.

She loves speaking to passionate groups of educators. You can connect with Allyson on Twitter, Instagram, and Facebook at @AllysonApsey, through her website, AllysonApsey.com, or via email at AllysonApsey@gmail.com.

BRING ALLYSON
TO YOUR DISTRICT
OR ORGANIZATION!

Allyson is a dynamic national speaker who fills the room with energy. She specializes in captivating presentations that are emotional journeys for all present. The participants laugh, cry, get surprised, and reflect throughout their time together. The interactive format is engaging, fun, and inspiring. There is no doubt that participants walk out of Allyson's keynotes or presentations changed. They discover new perspectives, new goals, and strategies to implement right away.

Popular topics from Allyson Apsey:

- Leading the Whole Teacher
- Supporting Students, Staff, and Families Affected by Trauma
- Helping Others Discover the Best in Themselves
- Flipping the Script for Staff Meetings: Creating a Culture of Collaboration
- Evaluation as a Teacher Empowerment Tool
- HANDLE-ing Each Other with Care
- Discovering the Path to Serendipity
- Leading from the Inside Out
- Creating Need-Satisfying Environments Where People Thrive
- Building Strong, Positive Relationships

Contact Allyson via email at AllysonApsey@gmail.com.

MORE FROM
DAVE BURGESS Consulting, Inc.

Since 2012, DBCI has published books that inspire and equip educators to be their best. For more information on our titles or to purchase bulk orders for your school, district, or book study, visit DaveBurgessConsulting.com/DBCIbooks.

Like a PIRATE™ Series
Teach Like a PIRATE by Dave Burgess
eXPlore Like a PIRATE by Michael Matera
Learn Like a PIRATE by Paul Solarz
Plan Like a PIRATE by Dawn M. Harris
Play Like a PIRATE by Quinn Rollins
Run Like a PIRATE by Adam Welcome
Tech Like a PIRATE by Matt Miller

Lead Like a PIRATE™ Series
Lead Like a PIRATE by Shelley Burgess and Beth Houf
Balance Like a PIRATE by Jessica Cabeen, Jessica Johnson, and Sarah Johnson
Lead beyond Your Title by Nili Bartley
Lead with Appreciation by Amber Teamann and Melinda Miller
Lead with Culture by Jay Billy
Lead with Instructional Rounds by Vicki Wilson
Lead with Literacy by Mandy Ellis
She Leads by Dr. Rachael George and Majalise W. Tolan

Leadership & School Culture

Beyond the Surface of Restorative Practices by Marisol Rerucha

Change the Narrative by Henry J. Turner and Kathy Lopes

Choosing to See by Pamela Seda and Kyndall Brown

Culturize by Jimmy Casas

Discipline Win by Andy Jacks

Escaping the School Leader's Dunk Tank by Rebecca Coda and Rick Jetter

Fight Song by Kim Bearden

From Teacher to Leader by Starr Sackstein

If the Dance Floor Is Empty, Change the Song by Joe Clark

The Innovator's Mindset by George Couros

It's OK to Say "They" by Christy Whittlesey

Kids Deserve It! by Todd Nesloney and Adam Welcome

Let Them Speak by Rebecca Coda and Rick Jetter

The Limitless School by Abe Hege and Adam Dovico

Live Your Excellence by Jimmy Casas

Next-Level Teaching by Jonathan Alsheimer

The Pepper Effect by Sean Gaillard

Principaled by Kate Barker, Kourtney Ferrua, and Rachael George

The Principled Principal by Jeffrey Zoul and Anthony McConnell

Relentless by Hamish Brewer

The Secret Solution by Todd Whitaker, Sam Miller, and Ryan Donlan

Start. Right. Now. by Todd Whitaker, Jeffrey Zoul, and Jimmy Casas

Stop. Right. Now. by Jimmy Casas and Jeffrey Zoul

Teachers Deserve It by Rae Hughart and Adam Welcome

Teach Your Class Off by CJ Reynolds

They Call Me "Mr. De" by Frank DeAngelis

Thrive through the Five by Jill M. Siler

Unmapped Potential by Julie Hasson and Missy Lennard

When Kids Lead by Todd Nesloney and Adam Dovico

Word Shift by Joy Kirr

Your School Rocks by Ryan McLane and Eric Lowe

Technology & Tools

50 Things to Go Further with Google Classroom by Alice Keeler and
Libbi Miller

50 Things You Can Do with Google Classroom by Alice Keeler and
Libbi Miller

140 Twitter Tips for Educators by Brad Currie, Billy Krakower, and
Scott Rocco

Block Breaker by Brian Aspinall

Building Blocks for Tiny Techies by Jamila "Mia" Leonard

Code Breaker by Brian Aspinall

The Complete EdTech Coach by Katherine Goyette and Adam Juarez

Control Alt Achieve by Eric Curts

The Esports Education Playbook by Chris Aviles, Steve Isaacs,
Christine Lion-Bailey, and Jesse Lubinsky

Google Apps for Littles by Christine Pinto and Alice Keeler

Master the Media by Julie Smith

Raising Digital Leaders by Jennifer Casa-Todd

Reality Bytes by Christine Lion-Bailey, Jesse Lubinsky, and
Micah Shippee, PhD

Sail the 7 Cs with Microsoft Education by Becky Keene and
Kathi Kersznowski

Shake Up Learning by Kasey Bell

Social LEADia by Jennifer Casa-Todd

Stepping Up to Google Classroom by Alice Keeler and
Kimberly Mattina

Teaching Math with Google Apps by Alice Keeler and
Diana Herrington

Teachingland by Amanda Fox and Mary Ellen Weeks

Teaching with Google Jamboard by Alice Keeler and
Kimberly Mattina

Teaching Methods & Materials

All 4s and 5s by Andrew Sharos

Boredom Busters by Katie Powell

The Classroom Chef by John Stevens and Matt Vaudrey

The Collaborative Classroom by Trevor Muir

Copyrighteous by Diana Gill

CREATE by Bethany J. Petty

Deploying EduProtocols by Kim Voge, with Jon Corippo and Marlena Hebern

Ditch That Homework by Matt Miller and Alice Keeler

Ditch That Textbook by Matt Miller

Don't Ditch That Tech by Matt Miller, Nate Ridgway, and Angelia Ridgway

EDrenaline Rush by John Meehan

Educated by Design by Michael Cohen, The Tech Rabbi

The EduProtocol Field Guide by Marlena Hebern and Jon Corippo

The EduProtocol Field Guide: Book 2 by Marlena Hebern and Jon Corippo

The EduProtocol Field Guide: Math Edition by Lisa Nowakowski and Jeremiah Ruesch

The EduProtocol Field Guide: Social Studies Edition by Dr. Scott M. Petri and Adam Moler

Expedition Science by Becky Schnekser

Frustration Busters by Katie Powell

Fully Engaged by Michael Matera and John Meehan

Game On? Brain On! by Lindsay Portnoy, PhD

Guided Math AMPED by Reagan Tunstall

Innovating Play by Jessica LaBar-Twomy and Christine Pinto

Instructional Coaching Connection by Nathan Lang-Raad

Instant Relevance by Denis Sheeran

Keeping the Wonder by Jenna Copper, Ashley Bible, Abby Gross, and Staci Lamb

LAUNCH by John Spencer and A.J. Juliani

Learning in the Zone by Dr. Sonny Magana

Lights, Cameras, TEACH! by Kevin J. Butler

Make Learning MAGICAL by Tisha Richmond

Pass the Baton by Kathryn Finch and Theresa Hoover

Project-Based Learning Anywhere by Lori Elliott

Pure Genius by Don Wettrick

The Revolution by Darren Ellwein and Derek McCoy

Shift This! by Joy Kirr

Skyrocket Your Teacher Coaching by Michael Cary Sonbert

Spark Learning by Ramsey Musallam

Sparks in the Dark by Travis Crowder and Todd Nesloney

Table Talk Math by John Stevens

Unpack Your Impact by Naomi O'Brien and LaNesha Tabb

The Wild Card by Hope and Wade King

Writefully Empowered by Jacob Chastain

The Writing on the Classroom Wall by Steve Wyborney

You Are Poetry by Mike Johnston

Inspiration, Professional Growth & Personal Development

Be REAL by Tara Martin

Be the One for Kids by Ryan Sheehy

The Coach ADVenture by Amy Illingworth

Creatively Productive by Lisa Johnson

Educational Eye Exam by Alicia Ray

The EduNinja Mindset by Jennifer Burdis

Empower Our Girls by Lynmara Colón and Adam Welcome

Finding Lifelines by Andrew Grieve and Andrew Sharos

The Four O'Clock Faculty by Rich Czyz

How Much Water Do We Have? by Pete and Kris Nunweiler

P Is for Pirate by Dave and Shelley Burgess

A Passion for Kindness by Tamara Letter

The Path to Serendipity by Allyson Apsey

Rogue Leader by Rich Czyz

Sanctuaries by Dan Tricarico

Saving Sycamore by Molly B. Hudgens

The SECRET SAUCE by Rich Czyz

Shattering the Perfect Teacher Myth by Aaron Hogan

Stories from Webb by Todd Nesloney

Talk to Me by Kim Bearden

Teach Better by Chad Ostrowski, Tiffany Ott, Rae Hughart, and Jeff Gargas

Teach Me, Teacher by Jacob Chastain

Teach, Play, Learn! by Adam Peterson

The Teachers of Oz by Herbie Raad and Nathan Lang-Raad

TeamMakers by Laura Robb and Evan Robb

Through the Lens of Serendipity by Allyson Apsey

The Zen Teacher by Dan Tricarico

Children's Books

Alpert by LaNesha Tabb

Alpert & Friends by LaNesha Tabb

Beyond Us by Aaron Polansky

Cannonball In by Tara Martin

Dolphins in Trees by Aaron Polansky

I Can Achieve Anything by MoNique Waters

I Want to Be a Lot by Ashley Savage

Micah's Big Question by Naomi O'Brien

The Princes of Serendip by Allyson Apsey

A Teacher's Top Secret Confidential by LaNesha Tabb

A Teacher's Top Secret: Mission Accomplished by LaNesha Tabb

Ride with Emilio by Richard Nares

The Wild Card Kids by Hope and Wade King

Zom-Be a Design Thinker by Amanda Fox